Sally Edwards

The Heart Rate Monitor
GUIDEBOOK
To Heart Zone Training

SMART HEART

First Printing: June 1999
Printed in Australia

Published in South Australia by: **Performance Matters Pty Ltd**
308 Carrington Street, Adelaide SA 5000 Australia
Phone: (08) 8223 2077 • Fax: (08) 8223 3855
Email: nunan@enternet.com.au
http://www.pursuit-performance.com.au

Printed by: **Bowden Printing Pty Ltd**
"Troon House", 26 Hindmarsh Ave, Welland SA 5007 Australia

Layout by: **Image & Substance Pty Ltd**
308 Carrington Street, Adelaide SA 5000 Australia

This book is available at quantity discounts for bulk purchases or special editions. For information call (08) 8223 2077.

I offer the advice in this book to people who are not ill and who have no serious medical problems that require professional or medical care. Any readers who experience any sort of physical, emotional or mental problems should consult a doctor immediately.

TABLE OF CONTENTS

This book is dedicated

To all exercisers, athletes,

fitness professionals, individuals

in the medical profession,

teachers and coaches

To my training partners

To my business partners

To Performance Matters because

it matters that we perform.

Our differences

It's wonderful that sport and training are the same.

But, our spelling is sometimes different.

This book was written in American English and

edited into Australian English.

Please enjoy both and accept our spelling differences.

 HRM GUIDEBOOK BY SALLY EDWARDS

INTRODUCTION
by Neil Craig

When browsing through general health or sporting magazines there is a very real chance you will encounter articles or advertisements depicting why you should purchase and use a heart rate monitor during your exercise program. For the general exercise enthusiast we are told that safety, motivation and optimal return in fitness for your valuable expenditure of exercise time are all valid reasons to purchase this fantastic piece of exercise equipment. For the more serious performer we are told the heart rate monitor can give you that edge over your opposition.

Of course, all the above is true. Unfortunately, the majority of what is written or advertised about heart rate monitors is about the hardware, i.e., what it can measure, the specifications, the features and its appearance and style. Very little is written about the "software", i.e., information about how to make the heart rate monitor work best for you. What heart rate should I be aiming for if I want to maximize fat loss? How do I know whether I am recovering between exercise sessions? What heart rate levels should I be aiming to hold for during next week's marathon? Has my fitness level improved over the last 6 weeks of training?

So you have the hardware, where do you get the software? Enter Sally Edwards and "The Heart Rate Monitor Guidebook"!

I first had the privilege of meeting Sally at a "Heart Zone Training" seminar that we co-conducted in Australia in 1998. As she delivered her scientific and practical knowledge on how to use the flashing digital number on the screen of your heart rate monitor, it soon became obvious that Sally was the "software" that people had been looking for. Here was a person who actually knew how to use a heart rate monitor.

For the past 15 years I have worked and trained with some of the best coaches and athletes in the world. During this time we have successfully applied heart rate monitor technology to areas of competition, training, recovery, testing and research; all for an improvement in performance. That's why the majority of our Olympic athletes have their own heart rate monitor (or access to one) and that's why I continually urge other coaches to do the same with their athletes. But remember, the techniques I use with the elite athlete are no different than the techniques I would use with you. Yes that's right, the same technology and techniques will work for you, even though you don't have a coach and you aren't an Olympic athlete. There are no hidden secrets or formulas; it's all about knowing how to use that digital number on the heart rate monitor screen - it's about having the software!

As a result of Sally's latest book, "The Heart Rate Monitor Guidebook", we all now have access to Sally's "software". If you have purchased a heart rate monitor it is a book you must have. If you are unsure about the value a heart rate monitor can have for your program, "The Heart Rate Monitor Guidebook" will leave you in no doubt that with the combination of a heart rate monitor and the appropriate software, you will now have your own personal trainer.

Irrespective as to whether you're about to begin an exercise program or whether you're a highly competitive athlete, "The Heart Rate Monitor Guidebook" contains information that will enable you to maximise the performance of your heart rate monitor and your exercise program. It is easy to read and you will certainly relate to the many examples and experiences quoted in the book. However, most importantly an experienced professional who knows her business has written it.

Neil Craig
Author of Scientific Heart Rate Training
Exercise Physiologist, Sports Science Coordinator for the Australian Cycling Federation

The Forward to Heart Zone Training

by Sally Edwards

Thanks for selecting *The HRM Guidebook* and opening up your new path to fitness and personal fulfilment.

Heart Zone Training works. It doesn't matter if you've started exercise programs and quit a hundred times. It doesn't matter if you've started just as many diets and been frustrated time and again by the "yo-yo" effect. The promise here is a reality.

A reliable, accessible fitness program has been a long time coming. Since 1968, when Dr. Ken Cooper wrote his pivotal exercise book, *Aerobics,* the idea of fitness through exercise has been in the air. Cooper sent millions into motion, and it was an excellent first step, a great kick-off to the movement. He was followed by hundreds more best-selling/worst-delivering fitness authors, video-exercise queens, and equipment gadgeteers who promised the dream and delivered only short-term results.

They and we have failed, and it's only just now becoming clear why. Our failure was rooted in one basic premise (maybe it'd be more accurate to call it a "conceit," since wasn't that what those effortlessly fit diet/exercise gurus always seemed, *conceited*?): that what works for one person, who just happens to be an athlete, works for us *all*. In fact, as you well know, it didn't work, and the net effect is what we see today: people getting more sedentary, less fit, and with little or no hope that they *can* get fit, ever.

We've been through the "you-only-have-to-diet" plan and the "you-only-have-to-exercise" plan. Both of these became monsters on the loose in the hearts and minds of men, women, and even children, succeeding in chewing up the thing we could

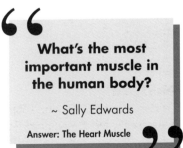

What's the most important muscle in the human body?

~ Sally Edwards

Answer: The Heart Muscle

least afford to lose: our hope. There's no mystery to this sad process - when you don't get results, you lose hope, and losing hope keeps you from trying again in the future. None of us want to get fooled again.

I'd like to offer you, my readers, an honest program that makes sense, a dose of hope for the weary and cynical. I still believe that everyone can become who they want to be physically, emotionally and spiritually. Why? Because I've seen Heart Zone Training *work*. Now, I don't believe that it's going to work for those who are too cynical (or lazy!) to even try to help themselves, but I do believe I can show you the common sense of this program and give those sincere folks who've lost their hope another chance.

Heart Zone Training works. Guaranteed. It's so much guaranteed that if you can't follow the book or find that it doesn't deliver on its promise, I'll give you a no-questions-asked refund. It's that solid a program.

What this program offers are the tools, the instructions, the data, and the support for you to make and reach your *personal* goals.

We've done our best to make this journey easy for you. Through the use of icons that appear in the margin, information of special interest-such as losing weight, getting healthier, aerobic fitness, or high performances training is highlighted so you can skip from key point to key point as best fits your needs. Or, of course, you can sit down and read The HRM Guidebook all the way through.

You can consider Heart Zone Training to be one more vehicle on the information superhighway, but this isn't any plodding bus filled with an uneven mix of passengers coming from and going to who knows where, whose final destination is at the whim of some distant corporation or uninterested driver. Heart Zone Training is a brand-new, high-speed electric train, whose cars *split off* at the rider's request, becoming personal vehicles which conduct you to within feet of your goal, not miles.

We swim in the midst of a flood of fitness information these days, but the key to avoiding being swept away by it is to remember that if it doesn't fit, if it's not tailored to *your* personal needs, then it's not going to take you where *you* want to go.

Consider The HRM Guidebook your personal rescue vehicle, set on the course of your lifetime fitness. Bon Voyage.

Sally Edwards, Author, Athlete, Business-person
Sacramento, California 1997… www.HeartZone.com

Also by Sally Edwards...

- *The Heart Rate Monitor Guidebook to Heart Zone Training,* Performance Matters, 1999
- *Caterpillars to Butterflies,* Heart Zones, 1997
- *Heart Zone Training,* Adams Media, 1996
- *Snowshoeing,* Human Kinetics, 1995
- *The Heart Rate Monitor Book,* Polar Electro Oy, 1993
- *Triathlons for Fun,* Triathlete Magazine, 1992
- *Triathlons for Women,* Triathlete Magazine, 1992
- *Triathlons for Kids,* Triathlete Magazine, 1992
- *The Equilibrium Plan: Balancing Diet and Exercise for Lifetime Fitness,* Arbor House, 1987
- *Triathlon Training and Racing Book,* Contemporary Books, 1985
- *Triathlon: A Triple Fitness Sport,* Contemporary Books, 1982

Your First Seven Steps

Physical activity is one of life's most individual pursuits. Regardless of whether you exercise in a group or by yourself, working out is still ultimately about you being motivated by your own personal reasons to be physically active. You might want to get healthy, you might want to stay fit, or you might want to get still fitter. Still, many people have found they work out better with others - a running group, a personal trainer, a team and/or coach, an exercise physiologist - so they can get on-the-spot feedback and motivation for their fitness efforts.

This is where using a heart rate monitor (some prefer to call it a "heart rate monitor") can be so important. When you've got a heart rate monitor, it doesn't matter if you are working out alone or with a group, you now have an extremely reliable, precise source of feedback. With a heart rate monitor, you can be your own best motivator, your own personal trainer, your own exercise physiologist! People around the world are discovering that a heart rate monitor is the best workout partner they've ever had.

The heart rate monitor provides a seamless link between your body and your mind. No more wracking your brain as you try to guess your exercise intensity, no more stopping in the middle of an aerobic session to search desperately for your pulse, hoping to get a reasonably close count before your heart rate starts to plummet. For years professional athletes have had access to this kind

> **"You only need two pieces of gear to workout: a good pair of athletic shoes and a heart rate monitor.**
>
> ~ Sally Edwards **"**

of information, but now this potent training tool is available to everyone. You, too, now have real training power.

So, whether you are in training with a clear-cut fitness goal, or are exercising for your health or the pure joy of sport, having a heart rate monitor means you can do so more simply and efficiently. Training with your watch will help you better enjoy your exercise or more quickly reach your goal. And when you add to your new tool the information on heart zone training, you are on your way to enjoying each and every moment of physical activity, stretching your body to new places and, in turn, stretching your mind.

Heart zone training with your mind-body link – the heart rate monitor - may seem confusing at first. You'll be learning and discovering new ways of looking at the effort you put out, new ways of understanding fitness, that you were never taught in your physical education classes at school. A lot has happened in the world of fitness in just the last ten years, and with your heart rate monitor and heart zone training, you are ready to reap the benefits.

The first step to take with your heart rate monitor is easy: strap it on!

STEP 1. TAKE THE 24-HOUR EXPERIENCE

To start, simply wear your heart rate monitor continuously for 24 hours so that you can learn to use it as a feedback monitor. See that heart flashing in the face of the watch? That's your heart actually beating. Stare at the face of the monitor for a couple of minutes. Check to see that every beat at rest is evenly spaced, the heart icon that flashes does so with complete regularity.

Wear your heart rate monitor when you first wake up in the morning and note the number it shows. This is your heart rate at rest or your "resting heart rate." Notice how your heart rate changes from when you are lying in bed to when you are sitting up and walking around. Check out your heart rate when you are in the middle of your day, sedentary and relaxed. That's your ambient heart rate. Note what happens if you get excited or stressed – emotionally, not physically. Does your heart rate change?

Watch as you move around doing different tasks. Do your regular workout and just observe the movement of the numbers. Get an idea of what the highest reading is during your workout. Is it over 100 beats per minute (bpm) or under? If you made it over 100 bpm, note how long it takes for you to break 100 bpm going back down, by resting after you quit exercising. That's a measure of how good your recovery heart rate is. After a day of this, you'll definitely find that your heart rate will increase and decrease as you increase and decrease your efforts or training load.

"Training Load" is a key idea. It is, by definition, the amount of F.I.T. you do. What does F.I.T. mean? That acronym stands for frequency, intensity, time, and when all three are put together it's called training load. Frequency is how often you are exercising. Intensity means how hard you are training (or, as you'll see, in what heart zones). And time refers to how long you are exercising.

Here's a bulletin: scientific research is now in that says it doesn't so much matter how long or how frequently you exercise. What most matters is the quality of your workouts, their intensity. The additional good news is that we now know that harder intensity isn't always better; rather the opposite is often true. Depending on your goals, the easier you go, the more results you may get. In addition, the easier you go at first, the better the odds that you'll still be exercising on a regular basis after an extended period of time. Those who quit training programs most frequently are those who push themselves into too high a training load. They work out too hard, too long, too often. That's called burnout. So, go easy and use your heart rate watch to keep you in the lower heart rate ranges when you first start out.

That's it. You've passed your first experience - 24 hours of continuously using your heart rate monitor. After your first 24 hours of cardiac monitoring, you have probably learned a lot about how your heart

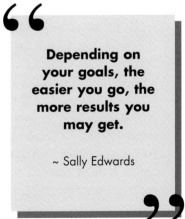

> **Depending on your goals, the easier you go, the more results you may get.**
>
> ~ Sally Edwards

responds to your different daily activities. You may have also found that your heart rate watch is not only a source of feedback on your physical activities but is also a source of emotional feedback. Did you get angry in traffic or at the television or thrilled by a phone call from a long-missed friend? If so, you may have noticed the effects of emotional stress on your heart rate. In fact, long-time users of heart rate watches often praise these tools just as much for their ability to remind the wearer to stay emotionally calm as for the monitors ability to motivate users to put out their best fitness efforts!

STEP 2. LEARN TO PROGRAM YOUR HEART RATE MONITOR

Every heart rate monitor works differently, with the functional details dependent on the model. The first step for all users, though, might be to understand the difference between a heart rate monitors and a heart rate watch. While all heart rate watches are heart rate monitors, not all heart rate monitors are heart rate watches. The difference is easy to see. Does your monitor include a readout with the time of day? If it does, then it's a heart rate watch. That's why people talk about heart rate watches and monitors as if they were the same thing – they're not, and now you know why. (For our purposes in this book a heart rate watch and a rate monitor will be considered the same thing.)

So, your heart rate monitor just replaced your time of day watch by giving you both the time and your heart rate in one convenient place. The first thing to do then is to set the correct time of day on your new tool (or your new *toy*, as a lot of people think of it!). This may take you as little as one minute or as many as thirty, but spending the time right now with your instruction booklet and watch is your best investment. You want your heart rate monitor to become your best friend, and it can only be that if you learn how to get comfortable with programming it. This means sharing some of your time with the instruction booklet packaged with most monitors.

Along with setting the time, you'll see that most heart rate monitors also work as stop watches. Try starting and stopping it a few times until you feel confident, since this is a handy feature for measuring the length of your workouts.

Now that you know how to start and stop your stop watch and how to set your time of day, it's time to understand the heart-oriented functions of your watch. Heart rate monitor features are designed around the concept of heart zones. That's a new term and you might want to jump to the sidebar at the end of this chapter for definitions or go to Step #3 to learn more. For now, know that the key purpose of the heart rate functions is to provide you with a range (or "zone") of heart beats in which you exercise. The upper limit of this range is called your ceiling and your lower limit is the floor. Learn how to set your upper ceiling and the lower floor of your heart zone by reading the instruction manual. Memorise this procedure.

Next, learn how to turn on and off the alarm feature. The alarm sounds when you are above your ceiling or below the floor of your zone. If you work out too hard and your heart rate exceeds the top number or upper limit of your zone, an alarm will sound to let you know. Likewise, if you exercise too gently and drop below your floor, the same alarm will sound and tell you that.

Some models have additional and important features. First, your watch might have a back lighting feature which allows you to see the face of the monitor easily when it's dark. You may also have a countdown timer; you can have your watch count backwards for up to three hours and set off a beeper when it reaches zero. The heart monitor part of your tool/toy also might have two new features: heart rate memory and heart rate recall.

Heart rate memory is important because it measures your "time in zone." Your goal is to set the ceiling and floors of your heart rate zone and stay within those boundaries for the workout. But if you go outside the zone limits, above or below, it is going to remember how much time you spent out of zone. Heart rate recall is your download function. After the workout or timed event, you can push the recall button and the heart watch will give you the time spent above your zone, within your selected heart zone, and below it.

All of this is done within 99% of the accuracy of a full EKG machine - the kind you see for cardiac monitoring in a medical environment - without the hassle of being laid out on a table and strapped to a large, immobile machine, and without the incredible expense. Now you know that for every workout from here on in, your first step will be to program your heart zones for that workout and turn on your alarm. If you follow this discipline you can train less time, with more precision and gain the benefit from training in zones.

STEP 3. USE THE FIVE TRAINING ZONES

Before reading this book, you may have already heard about something called a target heart zone. Well, I'm here to tell you that the single, set, target heart zone doesn't exist. There is no one zone, no one range of heart rates, that is best for everyone. Each of our bodies are different and each of our fitness/training goals are different, so there are multiple, different, zones. And in each of these different zones you get different benefits; or, as some say, multiple zones beget multiple benefits.

WELLNESS HEART ZONE CHART

Zone Number	Zone Name	% Maximum Heart Rate	Benefit of Zone
#1	Health Zone	50%-65%	For getting fit
#2	Fitness Zone	65%-80%	For staying fit
#3	Performance Zone	80%-100%	For getting your fittest

Each of the zones is named for the benefits that you get from exercising within them.

The heart zone chart shows us a few important things. One, as mentioned above, there are multiple zones. Two, each of the heart zones is determined by a percentage of your maximum heart rate. Three, by working out in different zones you receive different benefits.

TRAINING HEART ZONE CHART

Zone Number	Zone Name	% Maximum Heart Rate	Benefit of Zone
Z 1	Healthy Heart Zone	50%-60%	For getting fit
Z 2	Temperate Zone	60%-70%	For staying fit
Z 3	Aerobic Zone	70%-80%	For getting fitter
Z 4	Threshold Zone	80%-90%	For getting even more fit
Z 5	Redline Zone	90%-100%	For getting fittest

STEP 4. KNOW YOUR MAXIMUM HEART RATE

You may already have noticed the next key idea: your maximum heart rate. So what is it? Your maximum heart rate by definition is the greatest number of times your heart can make within a one-minute period. Your heart will only contract so fast and not one beat faster – that's why it's called your maximum heart rate. Your maximum heart rate is also a fixed number, and you should know that everyone's maximum heart rate is different. Two individuals who are both fifty years old could have a difference as high as 40 beats between their maximum heart rates.

There are a couple of ways of testing to determine your true maximum heart rate. The one I use most often is just to find the highest number you ever observe on your monitor when exercising and call that number your maximum. Others like to use the "talk test," which is to exercise until you find talking uncomfortable and then add 30-40 bpm to that number, resulting in a guesstimate of your maximum. Another way for you to approximate your maximum is by using a mathematical equations. One of the more reliable is the following:

Maximum Heart Rate Calculation

210 - (half your age) - (.05 x your weight)

+ 4 (if you're male; females don't add anything).

Here's an example for a 150-pound woman and 200-pound man who are both age 50.

Woman: 210 - (1/2 x 50 years) - (.05 x 150 pounds)
= 210 -25 - 7 = 178 bpm max heart rate.

Man: 210 - (1/2 x 50 years) - (.05 x 200 pounds) + 4
= 210 - 25 - 10 + 4 = 179 bpm max.

♥ $\frac{MAX}{HR}$

Knowing your maximum heart rate ♥ $\frac{MAX}{HR}$ is important, so try the method that is most comfortable for you and use that number to set your zones. As you gain more experience, you'll get a more accurate estimation of your maximum, so be flexible and patient for now and allow that determining your maximum heart rate can be a challenge. Still, now that you have an approximate maximum, you are ready for the next step.

STEP 5. SET YOUR TRAINING HEART ZONES

Now that you have an idea of your maximum heart rate, you need to calculate your three heart zones: zone one, the Healthy Heart zone (50-65% max HR), zone two, the Fitness zone (65-80% max HR), and zone three, the Performance zone (80-100% max HR) or your five zones. To help you with these calculations, the Heart Zone Training chart on the following page will provide you with these numbers easily.

MAXIMUM HEART RATE SPHERE

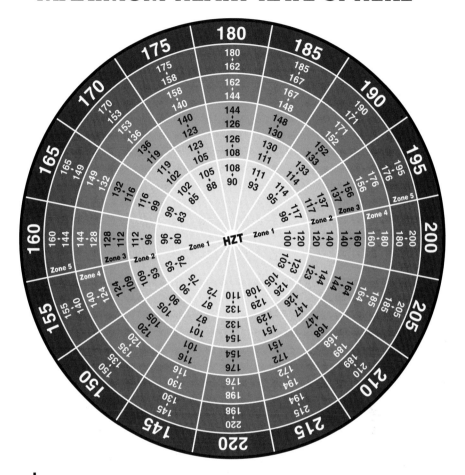

MAXIMUM HEART RATE SPHERE

To set your training heart zones, determine your maximum heart rate on the outer ring. Next, travel toward the centre point. As you cross each of the interior rings of the Maximum Heart Rate Sphere, you are entering a new heart zone. Each ring is 10% of your maximum heart rate. As you get closer to the centre point which is 50% of your maximum, it gets cooler, easier, light in intensity.

Now that you have toured through your Maximum Heart Rate Sphere, take charge of these five sets of numbers. Thay are yours. You should note the ceiling and floor of each of these zones, as those are the numbers that you are going to be using when you program your monitor. Your maximum doesn't change with age if you continue to be fit so you won't ever have to readjust your zones – they are yours for a near-lifetime.

STEP 6. START YOUR HEART ZONE TRAINING SYSTEM

You are ready.

You have everything you need to start your program: a heart rate watch, a maximum heart rate, your three to five heart zones. You can go out today and start exercising. But there are a few final tidbits of information which will help. First, it helps to know your time in zone. Keep track of how many minutes you train in which zones. If you are just beginning, start with 100% of your workout time in zone one, Healthy Heart. Stay in that zone for at least 2 to 4 weeks before you spend one single minute in zone two. Then, when zone one becomes easy and you are ready for the challenge, start with 10%-25% of your total training time in zone two. For example, if you are training four days a week for 20 minutes, then once a week put your zone two upper and lower limits in your monitor and train there. That would be three days in zone one and one day (that's 25%) in zone two. It's simple.

Next, all workout sessions should have the same general layout. You need to warm up by doing the specific activity slowly and gently until you have started to raise your heart rate level above your ambient numbers. For example, before I start a run, I always spend 10% of my total training time walking, as my warm up, and another 10% for my cool down, by walking again. I don't start by running during my first few minutes.

A typical workout of any length of time looks like the following:

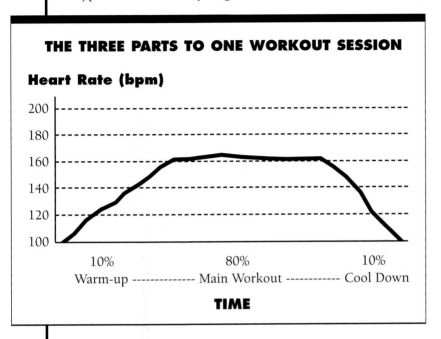

THE THREE PARTS TO ONE WORKOUT SESSION

Heart Rate (bpm)

200
180
160
140
120
100

10%   80%   10%
Warm-up -------------- Main Workout ------------ Cool Down

TIME

STEP 7. LOG YOUR WORKOUTS

It can help to motivate you and keep you on track to write down your workout. This is called keeping a training log, and you can create one of your own or use the one you'll find latter in this book. One of the important features of a log is that it gives you a place to record how much time you spent within your zone and how much time was above or below your training heart zone. Your goal is to stay in zone, remember, so if you hear that alarm sound because you are going too hard or easy just think of it as my voice, your heart zone training coach, telling you to slow down or to pick it up.

Another good reason to keep a log is to monitor your progress. There is a maxim that we follow as athletes and professionals:

You can manage best what you can measure and monitor.

That's what is so great about a heart rate watch. It is really your coach, your friend, your indicator of progress, your motivator – the most important piece of exercise equipment that you have ever used. Your new heart rate monitor is your management tool. It can measure your workouts, and it can monitor them while you are conducting them.

Everybody including fitness folks, athletes, personal trainers, coaches - everybody consider personal heart rate monitoring technology a powerful gift. It's changed our lives, and it can change yours. Use the power to make a difference in your life. Use the power to achieve your goals. Use the power to save you time. You've just made one of the most important purchases in your arsenal of power tools – now use it for every workout, as a biofeedback device, as your link between your mind and your heart. I do.

HEART RATE TERMS

Time Functions: The different type of timing features that a watch provides, such as the ability to display time of day or the ability to serve as a stop watch.

Heart Rate Functions: The different features that the heart rate watch provides, such as the ability to display current heart rate.

Heart Rate Monitor: An electronic device which measures the electrical activity of the heart and displays it.

Heart Rate Watch: An electronic device which combines a time of day watch with the features of a heart rate monitor in one unit.

Resting Heart Rate: The number of beats your heart contracts in sixty seconds when you first wake up, before you get out of bed.

Ambient Heart Rate: The number of beats per minute your heart contracts when you are awake but in a sedentary and stationary position.

Recovery Heart Rate: Heart rate after a set post exercise rest-interval such as 2 minutes.

Heart Zones: Different heart rate ranges which represent specific benefits that occur by exercising or training within their numeric limits.

Limits: The dividing lines of a heart zone – the top of a limit is the ceiling and the lowest point of a limit is its floor.

Exercise Heart Rate: The number of beats per minute as you are working out.

Average Heart Rate: Your mean heart rate for the entire exercise period   or session.

Peak Heart Rate: The highest heart rate number reached in one work-out period.

Anaerobic Threshold Heart Rate: That heart rate at the crossover from aerobic metabolism to anaerobic metabolism.

CHAPTER 2

The Five Basic Principles

Every fitness plan has the holy ground of principle: "Thou shalt not allow a cookie to cross thine lips"…"Thou shalt run 'til thou drop"…"Thou shalt suffer pain, then gain." Heart Zone Training, too, has its principles, but there are only five of them, and they're decidedly user friendly.

#1 YOUR SNEAKERS ARE FITTED; YOUR TRAINING SHOULD BE, TOO.

One size doesn't fit all. Yet we pick up books and magazines or turn on the television, and we see prepackaged programs that are guaranteed to work for everyone, from waif-like super models to gargantuan bodybuilders. And you, too. What's wrong with this picture?

And what about group exercise - all those aerobic classes or mass bicycle rides? Group exercise, historically, has always been the gold standard. Fill a swimming pool, a workout studio, a stadium or a gym with a group of exercisers and have them follow the leaders. Take an aerobics class - and we all have. Ever notice how the class breaks down into two groups? The ones at the front in the newest outfits - the fittest - compete with the instructor for the crispest move and least body fat; in the back are the ones struggling and just trying to survive. They're drooling from overwork, sweating like crazy, doing a harder workout because their training load is greater, struggling to catch up.

In-between these two groups are the poor folks who reluctantly got pushed forward from the back of the class or former front-of-the-classers who were forced back by absenteeism. All too frequently, before anyone gets out of the back or moves up to the front, she or he quits the exercise program. On the average, most last no more than 6 weeks in a group exercise class. Only a few do really well, and the rest just hang on.

Heart Zone Training is individualised training. Success is built around you and your abilities, interests, personality, and other important characteristics, such as body type, genetic make-up, mental stamina, and muscle structure.

What works for someone else may not work as well for you. What we want to do is to make Heart Zone Training fit your abilities and goals, because if we don't, success will always be just out of reach. Each of us is a whole person, with likes and dislikes, with limitations on our time.

Heart Zone Training is a program that is based on your individual fitness levels, your individual interests, your individual history, goals, needs, etc. It's totally about you. It allows you to move at your pace, and to get fit at your rate. Whether you want to accelerate that pace or keep the cruise control set, it's up to you, not the group leader.

The outcomes of individualised training are real and noticeable. Your benefits are based on goals you set and realise. The *doer* in you does what you enjoy, stimulating your interests. You start at whatever fitness level you're on and watch yourself improve, because you'll be seeing, feeling, touching, watching the metamorphosis of your body lead to your increased personal power.

As for time one of the greatest benefits of Heart Zone Training is that you'll get more fitness in less time. You can train as little as ten minutes a day and see measurable benefits. Now that's revolutionary!

#2 MULTIPLE ZONES GIVE MULTIPLE BENEFITS.

Remember all those charts on the walls of aerobics or weight rooms, charts listing our "target heart rate zone"? Good. Now forget them. If we want the individualised benefits of Heart Zone Training, we're going to forget about that single, set zone and concentrate instead on several smaller, more specific zones.

Why?

Because what we want from our training plan are multiple benefits - to be not only leaner, but stronger and healthier. It's great to fit into your clothes comfortably, to hear "hey, you look trim," to feel the inner satisfaction of accomplishing something as simple as running up a flight of stairs without breathing hard, to be able to keep up with your friends, and then give them that Cheshire smile that says it was easy.

Further more, despite what we might want, we live in a world of constrained time. We've all felt the frustration that comes from seeing people who don't have our time problems giving us advice on health and fitness. The simple fact is that few of us have unlimited time for exercise.

The only way to get the multiple benefits we desire in a realistic, *doable* amount of time is through an understanding of the multiple zones our hearts work through.

Heart Zone Training provides us with multiple benefits because, during the training, we will be exposing ourselves to multiple stimuli. One of the wonders of the human body is its uncanny ability to adapt to whatever stresses we throw at it. This is, of course, a two-edged sword. If the stresses we expose our bodies to are watching television and eating chips, we become very good at spectating and getting fat! But, if we expose the muscular system to resistance training, it adapts into this stronger model.

Back to those aerobic room charts. We told you to forget the "target heart rate zone" (which will be discussed) because there are, in fact, *five* training zones, each providing its unique benefits:

Numbering Your Zone

Percentage of Max Heart Rate	Zone Name	Zone Number
90%-100%	Redline Zone	Z 5
80%-90%	Threshold Zone	Z 4
70%-80%	Aerobic Zone	Z 3
60%-70%	Temperate Zone	Z 2
50%-60%	Healthy Heart Zone	Z 1

Within each training zone, different physiological activities - different stimuli to the body - occur. For example, if you want to get the health benefits of lower cholesterol and lower blood pressure, you need to train in the Healthy Heart zone, because those are the principle benefits of that zone. If you want to get faster as an athlete, you'll be spending at least some time in the Redline zone, an area that fitness folks rarely touch. When you're spending time in each of these different zones, you're accumulating the benefits of each one. These physiological and psycho-biological benefits include the metabolising of different fuels (i.e. burning fat and carbohydrates), strengthening sport-specific muscles, cardiovascularly conditioning different oxygen delivery systems, and training kinesthetic pacing skills.

The best part, is *you* get to choose what benefits *you* want, and *when*!

 ## YOU MANAGE BEST WHAT YOU CAN MEASURE AND MONITOR.

This simple statement has become a mantra for American business over the last few years, and it needs to be a personal mantra for every one of us. Why? Think about it; many of our so-called "failures" in diets and exercise programs stem from our inability to accurately monitor the changes we hope are taking place. The classic example, of course, is starting a training program to build muscle and using only our bathroom scales as the yard-stick of success or failure. Muscle mass weighs more than fat, so even though the program may be succeeding - our clothing getting looser and looser, our bodies feeling stronger and stronger - our monitoring device tells us to "forget it"!

Given the number of things in our lives that are neither con-trollable nor measurable, it's surprising that Heart Zone Training is both. You control it and you measure it.

The preferred tool for measuring and monitoring progress in Heart Zone Training is the heart rate monitor. With the use of this wireless device, you can continuously and instantaneously have information about your performance and your results. With this information and the intelligent interpretation of the information (which we will quickly teach you here), you can have a level of control that just a few years ago was available to only the most elite athletes. A heart rate monitor-based program measures and monitors your ongoing exercise experiences. A heart rate monitor is, quite simply, *the most powerful fitness and health tool available on the market today*. It's your personal power tool.

Can you do Heart Zone Training without a heart rate monitor?

Yes, you can, although it will be considerably more difficult - and subject to more error. If you don't have a heart rate monitor, watch closely for the hints and directions on manual monitoring and on other forms of heart rate testing we've included to guide you along the way.

The heart rate data that you're monitoring and measuring are the contractions of your heart muscle, measured in beats per minute. There are several important heart rate numbers, such as resting heart rate (Resting HR), ambient HR (also known as sitting heart rate) and maximum heart rate (Max HR).

And, unlike the pronouncements of those old-fashioned heart rate charts, your Max HR point does *not* necessarily decrease with age. There'll be more on this and other heart rate/fitness myths later.

#4 WELLNESS IS A CONTINUUM.

The great science fiction writer Ray Bradbury once wrote about, "the naming of names," the all-too-human urge to make sure everything has a handle for us to hold on to. We in the fitness industry are no different. In fact, think about the word "fitness." What does it mean, really? At its most basic, it can refer to cardiovascular fitness, muscular fitness, overall physical fitness or even mental fitness. A great word, but a little hard to tie down.

We have the same problem with "wellness," which is certainly more than the absence of disease. For our purposes, let's break wellness down into three areas, which when taken together form a continuum of good health and a critical aspect of Heart Zone Training.

The first component of wellness is one's basic (but not so basic when it's lacking!) health. For most of us, this is the key training area, because here we achieve the most essential health outcomes, such as weight management, lower cholesterol levels, and lower blood pressure. Training in the health area is usually at an easier activity level, where more fat as a percentage of total calories is burned. This is also the training area for those recovering from cardiovascular problems and undertaking cardiac rehabilitation. The two primary training zones in this area are the Temperate zone and the Healthy Heart zone.

for your information:

Of those who practice an exercise program as part of their cardiac rehabilitation, the reduction in the risk of death as a result is 20%.

The second component of aerobic wellness is fitness. When you're in this area, you're maintaining and improving your fitness, but this is measured by different parameters than it was in the health area. Aerobic fitness is measured as cardiovascular fitness, which is improved aerobic and anaerobic capacity. The exercise physiologists have lots of more precise terms for the fitness area: lactate tolerance enhancement, increased VO_2 capacity, improved anaerobic threshold heart rate, etc, etc. You can go to the back of this book for definitions of these terms - "Glossary of Heart Rate Terms". It suffices to say you can exercise harder or with more intensity than you could in the health area. Training in the fitness zone is strenuous but fun, challenging yet comfortable, and you can see body changes quicker than changes in the more basic health outcomes.

The third component in our wellness continuum is performance. This is where the athletes hang out, exercising with *high* heart rate numbers – all the way up to their max. The feeling is much different; you breathe hard and fast, you feel the burn in the sport-specific muscles, you see the blood vessels emerging to release heat, sometimes you even have a faint metal taste in your mouth from the anaerobic metabolic processes spewing out with high concentrations of lactates. *Whew!*

There are three different Wellness Zones within the heart zone training system which are a part of the five different zones. In the following chart, you can see how the health zone is within the bottom zones while the fitness zone is in the middle and the performance zones for athletes and competitors are the hotter and higher zones.

WELLNESS ZONES

Heart Zone Training Chart

Percentage of Max Heart Rate	Zone Name	Wellness Zone
90%-100%	Redline Zone	Performance Zone
80%-90%	Threshold Zone	Performance Zone
70%-80%	Aerobic Zone	Fitness Zone
60%-70%	Temperate Zone	Health Zone
50%-60%	Healthy Heart Zone	Health Zone

When you begin your individualised Heart Zone Training, you select which of these wellness areas you want to work in on any given day. Do you want:

- to improve your health, by lowering blood pressure and cholesterol levels and seeing weight loss or stability?
- to improve your fitness, as measured by improving your cardiovascular capacity?
- to improve your athletic performance, by raising your anaerobic threshold as close as possible to your Max HR?

Once you pick the one that suits you, then you know where you're going to spend time in heart zones.

 ## ZONE TRAINING IS A SYSTEM.

The KISS Principle (Keep It Simple, Stupid) isn't easy when we're talking about all the parts of the whole, then integrating that whole into our lifestyle. Yes, we guarantee that Heart Zone Training will work for you, but maybe we'd better throw another old saying into the mix: "There's no such thing as a free lunch."

You are going to have to work the plan to make the plan work for you.

But don't forget that you have a "secret weapon" on your side - a proven methodology hooked to a modern training tool, the heart rate monitor, which together produce results. As your body and mind link with the accurate and reliable information from your monitor, you're able to achieve the small goals that, combined, lead incrementally to the big one.

This system permits you to effectively integrate the different parts of your lifestyle. Without drifting into metaphysics, Heart Zone Training encourages you to see yourself as a whole person and act accordingly; it's as much about the mind as it is about the body. You can fret endlessly about which controls which, or you can just watch the two work in unison when the mind and body sides of the fitness equation are in balance.

Balance - that is the secret of Heart Zone Training. With the five-point canon, you can make Heart Zone Training a fitness lifestyle. The lifestyle offered here can take you to new levels of health, fitness, and performance. For those of us who live the lifestyle, it offers a deep feeling of fullfilment and happiness.

Workout #1:

THE Z1
HEART HEALTHY ZONE WORKOUT

Introduction. Each zone deserves its own example of a workout. Breaking through the aerobic floor is meaningful but you want to do so gently and allow your body to adjust to fitness. Start out with 10 minutes six days a week or 20 minutes three days a week for this workout is your choice. The body equates them as similar but not exact.

Workout Plan. Start by putting on a pair of walking shoes that are comfortable and wear some baggy street clothes. Choose a time of day which is most predictable so there are no distractions or competitions for your time. For most people, this is in the morning when there aren't opportunities throughout the day for planning another activity for that same time. Determine your specific numerical values for the Healthy Heart zone using the chart on page 19.

Workout. Stretch for a couple of minutes. Then start walking slowly and a minute later pick up the pace. It should take you about 60 seconds to break through the heart rate (HR) point which marks the floor or lower limit of the Z1 Healthy Heart zone. About every minute or two you need to take a quick glance at your monitor to make sure you are within the zone. For the last two minutes try to stay in the upper half of Zone 1. At the end of the two minutes slow down for about 60 seconds and let HR drop below your Zone 1 floor.

Comment. Ten minutes, that's all. Hang out here for several weeks and you'll begin to get fit. To get fitter you need to move up to the Z3 Aerobic zone and to get improved performance you need to exercise at least 25% of your time in the top two zones – Z5 Redline and Z4 Threshold.

The Heart Muscle
And Its Monitor

CHAPTER 3

Before we get into the dynamics of Heart Zone Training, we need to take a look at a couple of machines that are key to Heart Zone Training success. One is electronic - the heart rate monitor - the other, organic - the heart.

YOUR HEART

Everyone loves to use the heart to describe their own personal delight or despair. Poets talk about black hearts, bleeding hearts, and heart aches. Journalists use the heart to describe the cruel - heartless - and therapists want us to feel our emotions by getting connected to our inner heart. Doctors think of it as a plumber might-as a pump that sends liquids through pipes.

The heart is deeply tied to the rhythms of our lives as reflected in our language.

heart of the matter	change of heart
broken heart	in one's heart of hearts
steal one's heart	heart throb
halfheartedly	heavy heart
burning heart	heartless
purple heart	heartfelt
heart-rending	heart strings
heart-to-heart	after one's own heart

For now, we want to understand the very personal communication between the heart muscle and the heart monitor.

Each time your heart "beats" what it's really doing is going through one cycle of contraction and relaxation. The heart tells itself to do this by sending itself an electrical message. As the heartbeat begins, a positive electric charge spreads across the cell membranes. Then, there's a sudden change – the heart sends itself a negative charge that makes it contract. The heart's electrical change from the positive to the negative state is one heartbeat, and this electrical activity is what both heart rate monitors and electrocardiographs measure, allowing them to record your heartbeats very accurately.

for your information:

Don't confuse "pulse meters" with heart rate monitors - they are not the same thing! Heart rate monitors record your heart's electrical impulses, giving very accurate readings of your heart rate. Pulse meters, however, rely on light waves passing through the blood vessels (in your fingertip or earlobe, for example) for heart rate detection. Pulse meters are only fairly accurate when indoors and seated (like on an exercise bike) or at rest, and they are sensitive to changes in light in any situation. Compared to heart rate monitors, pulse meters simply aren't reliable or accurate enough - they're old technology.

YOUR HEART RATE MONITOR

As a sport snowshoe racer, some of my favourite moments have been spent standing in a warming hut out in the snowy back country. It's *cold* out there, shuffling along for miles on snowshoes. One day, standing in one such hut, the fire was just starting to warm me when I noticed my hut-mate, almost indistinguishable and certainly unidentifiable, covered head to toe in winter gear. "You're Sally Edwards," the voice said, "and I read your book. I win all of my races because I use the heart rate monitor like a weapon, and my competition doesn't."

"I know," I answered matter of factly. "So do I."

A heart rate monitor is a powerful tool. It reminds me of one of those plastic "Transformers" kids play with - I'm always finding new ways of using it. It can motivate you to do better, coach you or allow you to train yourself, sound off with cheeps and chirps to slow you down or pick you up, act as a testing device and even be your confidant and friend. Download your monitor into your personal computer to view your physical performance minute by minute, or use it in a race to challenge you not to get your heart rate too high or too low. Sometimes my heart rate monitor reads my mind, reflecting my emotional state in the rising and falling numbers on its face.

There are many different brands of heart rate monitors, each of which has many different models. Be advised that there are lots of choices and lots of options - microchips seem to trigger some sort of deep-seated "features-and-functions" urge in engineers. Everything is getting tech-ier with smaller monitors, cosmetically correct chest straps, all sorts of bells and whistles. What follows is a quick once-over of the basics.

THE PARTS OF A HEART RATE MONITOR

Heart rate monitors were in the realm of sci-fi not so very long ago. Researchers started checking heart rates around 1912, using water buckets as counterweights in the first laboratory model. The first electronic heart-monitoring tool, the electro-cardiograph, was originally the size of a room, and even today you would certainly not want to carry one around (even if you could afford one). Thankfully, today we have the personal heart rate monitor. It may not do everything the electrocardiograph in your doctor's office does, but it does very nicely fill the needs for anyone who wants to accurately measure their heart rate. Today's heart rate monitors are the size of a wrist watch at the price of a pair of top athletic shoes. Tomorrow, the heart rate monitor's computer electronics may integrate into a small fashion-smart watch with no electrode-bearing chest strap.

The names "heart rate monitor" and "heart rate watch" are synonymous. Most, but not all, monitors are watches. The monitor receives and collects the data transmitted from the chest strap and processes it through a computer chip to calculate a heart rate number. This number is updated every 3-5 seconds (or in real time with some monitors). The first few numbers that appear on your watch should be tossed out, because the software inside the computer needs enough sample heart rates to accurately calculate a value. Likewise, if you quickly accelerate or decelerate, your heart rate values will always be lagging behind your real heart rate number.

Attached to the elastic chest strap is the transmitter unit. The transmitter *receives* (okay, that's a little odd, but hang with us here) the data from our heart through its electrodes, processes it, then *transmits* it to the monitor.

for your information:
For more on heart rate monitors, jump to Appendix III in the back of the book and read on...

When I ran the Houston Marathon recently, my plan was to hold my heart rate at 162 bpm (beats per minute). Proving that Murphy's Law dares to operate even in Texas, my transmitter died at mile ten. Luckily, it wasn't one of those long, slow, agonising deaths – it just dropped dead at the 10 mile marker. At first I was devastated, running without my coach and without constant information. Then I passed through denial and depression, until the monitor miraculously came back to life.

I was joyous, but worried - the monitor read 182. Then it struck me - the fickle thing was picking up signals transmitted by the chest belt on the runner next to me! Boy, was <u>he</u> in trouble, but I needed that data. So I did the only logical thing - I asked him to pop off his transmitter and loan it to me. He just unsnapped his transmitter, let me snap it on for 60 seconds so I could compare pace with heart rate, and then I handed it back. I picked my pace up a few heartbeats to stay with him and, in return, he continued to loan me his transmitter. Thanks to the growing popularity of heart rate monitors, maybe we're evolving a whole new form of etiquette here. It's too early to tell, but you're free to contribute.

Now, strange readings are not the monitor's fault every time. What happened to my friend Heidi is a classic example. She called long distance recently in a stew. She perceived she was running at the same effort as always, but her heart rate was ten beats higher than usual. She thought the monitor had gone coo-coo and wanted me to tell her how to fix the watch.

for your information:
Edwards' Hint: If there are two people wearing transmitters within receiving distance of one another, the monitors may pick up both signals and add them together, or pick up your neighbour's signal, giving you a weird reading. Don't worry, you're not having some kind of coronary episode – just move away from your pal, or move your watch to your outside wrist. This is called "Cross Talk".

On my end, I was happy with the news, because that told me that her Heart Zone Training program was working. "Congratulations," I replied. "The readings might mean you're getting in shape, but let's do a test to be sure." I asked her to go run that favourite course of hers at that new heart rate and time herself. She phoned me back - this time thrilled. She ran her course five minutes faster, ten beats higher, but it didn't feel any more difficult. She was getting fitter. Her heart rate watch was her coach, and it helped her achieve her individual goal - getting faster.

Workout #2:
30-MINUTE WORKOUT FOR ANY SPORT

Introduction. The ratio of training load to rest or recovery is important in your training because it provides you with a way to progressively and systematically change the regimen by adding intensity which leads to training improvements.

Unfortunately, many athletes quantify the training load in broad, inexact simple terms like hard and easy. Your training will be more effective if you quantify the ratio of training load and rest in terms of training zones or even a specific heart rate point.

Purpose. To raise your anaerobic threshold heart rate (AT HR) using long intervals at specific HR points. (Note: For a definition of AT HR go to page 13).

Workout Plan. To do this 30-minute interval training session you must know your Max HR and AT HR. For this example we will use a Max HR of 200 bpm and AT HR of 175 bpm. The workout involves four-minute segments at 180 bpm or 90 percent Max HR (formerly known as "hard") and two-minute segments at 120 bpm or 60 percent Max HR (formerly known as "easy").

The Workout. After warming up adequately doing some form of cardiovascular exercise, accelerate quickly and steadily to 180 bpm and then hold this rate during the remaining portion of the four-minute period.

At the end of four minutes, quickly decelerate to 120 bpm and stay at that level for the remaining portion of the two minutes. Do five sets of four minutes at 180 bpm training load and two minutes at 120 bpm recovery for a total of 30 minutes. Finish with a warm down.

If you have a programmable heart rate monitor you can set the alarms at two minutes, a high HR limit of 180 bpm and a lower HR limit of 120 bpm. Using the stop watch and alarm functions, accelerate until you hear the upper limit alarm and then maintain until the four-minute mark, then slow down until reaching the lower limit alarm and hold until the two-minute mark.

Outcome. What you have accomplished is a long interval workout at or above the anaerobic threshold of most individuals. If you are in training to race, this workout plan should be a weekly regular. You can replace distance for time if you prefer to run by distance. You can also expand the duration progressively from 30 minutes to 36, 42 and 48 minutes.

Trapped Under A Paradigm

Much of how we relate to exercise and lifestyle changes is tied to our preconceived - and too often mistaken - notions, or paradigms, of how the body works. The heart rate monitor is the tool we use to shift our paradigms about exercise, about losing weight, about training. Like my friend Heidi, once we get objective information, we're able to change these notions.

PERCEPTION AND REALITY

What color is a can of that famous cola? Red, of course. Everybody knows that. But let's say you scuba dive to about 60 feet to look at that same cola can underwater. What color is it now? If you said, "Still red," you're wrong. The color we call "red" is a specific wavelength of light that bounces off objects painted or tinted to reflect that color. As it happens, this particular wavelength of light can't penetrate very deeply into water. The cola can isn't "red" when you see it lying in deep water because there is no red light that deep. But an interesting thing happens when divers do the above experiment – they *still* tend to see a red can. Our brains fill in the missing colour because we *know* that cola cans are red.

That's an example of the power of paradigms to determine how we look at the world. And, by the way, a paradigm can be as harmless as "all cola cans are red," or it can be as problematic as "no pain, no gain," or "no pain, no brain."

Our views of training are coloured by a set of accepted paradigms - the target heart rate, for example. "Target heart rate" sounds scientific, doesn't it? But, strangely enough, the target heart rate was never ferreted out by research, or proven by major experiments. It was, rather, a speculation number which, over the years, became accepted as gospel. Recently, the mythical target zone has grown wider and more cumbersome. The American College of Sports Medicine in *Guidelines for Exercise Testing and Prescription* enlarged it to 60%-90% of Max HR. This zone, once considered a window, is now a sliding glass door through which almost any activity can pass, allowing far too much variation for an individual (you!) to perform targeted training within.

ON THE BUS

In the summer of 1994, my troupe of travelling heart rate merrymakers journeyed to 14 cities in the U.S. with a seminar series to spread the word about Heart Zone Training. It reminded me of folk hero and author Ken Kesey when he and his cohorts hopped into their psychedelic-painted bus in the late '60s and travelled across America. The chemistry, of course, has changed. We've moved from the chemicals of the "Electric Kool-aid Acid Test" to self-generated endorphins. But one of Kesey's observations has stood the test of time: you're either on the bus or you're off the bus.

Either you get it or you don't. People across the country are struggling with a losing war on weight, looking for some faint glimmer of hope after the endless lack of success with fitness programs. They're beginning to think that fitness programs - like diets - don't work, and there's nothing that can or will.

The whole concept of a single target heart rate zone is tied up in those failures. On one particular stop early that summer, I was struck by the realisation that American fitness buffs, those professionals who were our seminar participants, couldn't give up the notion that there wasn't really a single target heart rate zone. This mythical zone was their entire aerobic belief system, their rock of Gibraltar. On this particular evening, I was lecturing at the Cooper's Aerobic Centre in Dallas, which is, in truth, the Mother Church of the whole aerobic movement.

That afternoon I toured the Cooper Centre facilities with one of their personal trainers. In the aerobics room, we came upon -

surprise! - a target heart rate chart posted on the wall. It was the *only* chart on the wall - that's how important it was to this aerobics room and to the aerobicisers' minds.

This wall chart showed age on the bottom axis and heart rate on the vertical axis, and how maximum heart rate and target training zone allegedly decline with age, based on the concept that, with each passing year, we get physiologically worse.

As I started to - politely, mind you - launch into my discourse of, "I want to tear down every one of these posters in every athletic club..." the trainer interrupted me.

"Sally, I'm embarrassed that we have these old posters on the wall. They're part of the *old* aerobic movement. We know the posters are wrong," he sheepishly admitted, "but we don't have anything to replace them with."

It made me realise that you can't take an entrenched belief system away from someone without replacing it with another belief system. That's the problem with paradigms. Having our existing paradigm disappear hurts and confuses us.

That chart also reminded me of how deeply entrenched the whole notion of age-predicted, maximum heart rates are; how many people have bought into the "220 minus your age" formula ("205 minus your age" for men) for determining their target heart rate.

That is a myth, a leftover paradigm from the days when we didn't know better. Fitness professionals and participants bought into it because it was universally preached to them, passed down from book to book, graduate to undergraduate, as if it were carved in stone. The sad part is that not only do these old systems not work, they leave people misguided.

I went to leading researcher Frank Katch, Ed.D., Professor of Exercise Science at the University of Massachusetts, in search of the origin of the mythical single training zone. Katch had asked me to stop by and teach his graduate students a seminar on heart rate monitors since my findings were revolutionary and exciting to him. On the front cover of one edition of his very popular college textbook, *Exercise Physiology*, was the same chart that was on the Cooper's Clinic wall in Dallas. Once again, the chart's importance was reflected in its position.

I asked where the chart originally came from, and Dr. Katch remarked that he had taken the chart from a textbook written by the professor before him. That professor probably borrowed it from *his* professor's textbook, and so on and so on. Like the Energiser Bunny, it just keeps going and going and going. And, it's a self-fulfiling prophecy that if we tell people their fitness is declining it gets worse.

Somewhere back there, this paradigm came from researchers. Without any other research method or data available at the time, they were forced to use statistics from cross-sectional studies of the population at large to predict Max HR. These early exercise scientists compared a group of 20 year-olds' Max HR with a group of 40 year-olds, and with a group of 60 year-olds. All the people were inactive. The researchers merely discovered that, in cross-sections of these populations, the Max HR dropped by about one beat per year.

Research is just now leaking out of the fitness labs from the first truly longitudinal research on Max HR. A longitudinal study is one that tracks the same cohorts of individuals over a long period of time, like 10 or 20 years. And what have these studies found? Surprise! In these studies, Max HR does not decline with age among those who maintain their fitness level. It only declines if they quit exercising.

for your information:
There are no longitudinal studies on changes in Max HR for women.

That's how myths grow. In this case, the entire fitness community believes in and has structured every single exercise program on a concept with no foundation - that there is a single target heart rate zone which is a percentage (typically 70%-85%) of a person's inaccurate, age-predicted, mathematically construed maximum heart rate. Rather, there are multiple zones which give you multiple benefits.

Time to take down those wall posters charts and get on the bus.

MAXIMUM HEART RATE

Maximum heart rate (Max HR) is the highest number of times per minute your heart can contract. This makes sense, doesn't it? It's the heart rate at the point of exhaustion in an all-out effort. You can continue to increase your intensity, but when you reach the Max HR point, your heart simply won't beat any faster. (Most researchers believe this genetically determined point is your body's way of protecting itself. If your heart beats too fast, it doesn't have enough time between beats to fill the chambers adequately, to fully contract and effectively pump the volume of blood needed to your body parts.)

There are at least a dozen mathematical equations to predict - guess - your maximum heart rate. Don't use any of them; they're all too inaccurate. Only a formula that uses your specific cardiovascular response can accurately predict your individual Max HR. (And we're going to provide you with several fun tests that can do just this, after more paradigm shifting.)

My search for supportive data on Max HR goes back to my UC Berkeley college notes. I found my class notes on maximum heart rate and target heart rate zone, now on yellowing pages. As students, we had to take lab work and test each other with everything from underwater weighing to various anthropometric measurements. Sure enough, there were my Max HR test results from 1969 as a 22-year-old coed - Sally Edwards' Max HR: 194 bpm.

Today, at the age of 50, my Max HR remains 194 bpm. It hasn't dropped a beat in 27 years.

Here's the pregnant "but": this is one woman's 26-year longitudinal study. One woman who has stayed in vigorous shape all the years. Today, I am 50 years old, and the most popular arithmetic formula calculates my Max HR to be 172 bpm (220 - 49). That's for a 23-point error.

Where did "220" come from? The number supposedly relates somehow to babies' Max HR. But there are no studies to support the idea that babies' maximum heart rates have been detected. (No one has found a way to get babies to run at top speed on a treadmill yet, I guess.)

for your information:

Children have smaller heart size and less total blood volume, which results in their having a lower stroke volume than an adult. To compensate, they have a higher heart rate for the same absolute workload.

♥ MAX HR

Using this antiquated technique of age-predicted Max HR, if a woman were 20 years old her age-predicted Max HR would be 200 beats per minute. Then, to set her heart rate zones, one would multiply the percentages as follows:

- 70% of 200 is 140 beats per minute
- 85% of 200 is 170 beats per minute
- Heart zone is a range of heartbeats between 140 bpm and 170 bpm or a 30 beat wide zone.

In fact, research has established there is an enormous margin of error for this formula - as great as thirty beats per minute. Quite frankly, that's just not accurate enough to work very well for very many people. Certainly it doesn't work for most people, and not at all for very active individuals.

Fact: 92% of Americans can't follow the exercise prescriptions recommended by the leading exercise scientific body, the American College of Sports Medicine (ACSM). Their 1990 exercise "position stand" suggests workouts 20 to 60 minutes long, at 60% to 90% (an enormous range!) of Max HR.

The bottom line is that this prescription that results in only 8% of the population exercising within this single zone notion has failed, and failed miserably. Frankly, the ACSM prescription does not address the needs and goals of each individual. A new guideline needs to be set and I expect that ACSM will release this soon.

for your information:

Fit women with the same body size have higher heart rates for the same workload as fit men. This is due to women's smaller left ventricle and lower blood volume, the result of males having more testosterone and it's effects on all muscles of the body.

TARGET HEART RATE

Busting some myths is harder than others. Busting the target heart rate theory is more difficult than keeping off the twenty pounds from the last diet. Few succeed at keeping the weight off, but we'll take a shot at target heart rates anyway.

The target heart rate zone is generally described as 70%-85% of your Max HR. This is the standard training zone or aerobic exercise prescription that is recommended by most professionals. The purpose of this one zone is an attempt to use important physiological criteria to set safe, simple, and effective training load dosages of exercise. The problem is having only that one zone. It still doesn't focus on or support benefits of Zone 1 and Zone 2 or Zone 4 and Zone 5.

A Quick Electronic Fountain of Youth

Determining an accurate Max HR is the key factor in setting your individual zones. To prove that let's look at my numbers:

	Max	70%	85%
Age Predicted:	170	119	145
Tested Max HR:	195	135	163
Error:	25	16	18

If I followed the age predicted formula, I wouldn't be able to run, I'd just have to walk to be able to stay at the low 120 bpm edge of the target zone, and I would not get enough exercise for my goals. I would be able to run at 146 bpm, but that pace is so easy for me that it's like being on cruise-control. I would be training too low to meet my racing objectives, and I would be terribly unhappy and unsatisfied. I'd probably quit. The error in all of the formulas is just too great - in my case, a 22 beat error in my Max HR is unacceptable because it would inappropriately limit my training regimen.

One of the only times that it is fun to have an inaccurate age-predicted Max HR is when I workout on a cardiovascular machine that is heart rate programmed and presets my zones for me if I give it my age. Because of the huge error in the arithmetic formula, I get to enter my age as 25 years old so it will set my zones correctly for my true Max HR.

When training at an athletic club in a Chicago suburb last year, I was testing a new cardio machine called the "Cross Trainer." The woman on the Cross Trainer next to me was in her mid-thirties and her control panel showed a heart rate reading of 195 bpm. She was working hard but not hurting herself. The HR number was flashing to indicate she was out of her machine-set target heart rate. I asked her how she felt about that large a heart rate number. She said, with great trepidation, "I am really, really worried that I am training too hard. But this is comfortable for me, and I don't know what else to do but do a workout that feels like I am accomplishing something and ignore the heart rate number." Clearly, she had a high true Max HR, and the age-predicted formula had failed her as it had failed me.

> **for your information:**
> A higher Max HR is not better than a lower Max HR.

The benefits of exercising below 70% of your Max HR are substantial. It is simple to understand why so few people have been successful at exercising particularly in the one zone - 70%-85% range - they haven't been told the correct information. Being able to get into a zone that is 70-85% Max HR is extremely difficult for the unfit to accomplish. It is too high and too strenuous, so why exercise when you can't do it anyway?

For people who are fit, the single zone is simply too easy. It may seem odd to people struggling to get into the zone, but one of the most common complaints at health clubs is, "I've been taking aerobics for one year - or two or three - and nothing is happening." It's also a complaint I hear from joggers, who are working hard, but not getting the results they anticipated.

The problem is the same for both groups: *there is no such thing as one target heart rate range.*

Do you want the truth? There are *multiple* zones that provide *multiple* benefits - not one zone for everyone. There are at least five different zones, and they are clearly identifiable by their physiological framework. The five zones are part of a continuum, beginning with the health zones, passing through the middle, fitness zone, and ranging all the way up to the performance zones.

QUICK TIP: A better way of describing "Target" Heart Rate is to call it a "Training" Heart Rate.

Perceived Level of Exertion (PLE)

So, why can't you tell yourself how hard you're working? (Hint: this is the next paradigm in need of a good, swift shift!) You ought to be able to do that, right? There's even a chart, called the rating of perceived exertion (RPE), that shows you how to correlate how you feel- your perceived exertion-to your heart rate. This sounds like you can plan to use the money saved on a heart rate monitor to buy frozen yogurt. But you'd better put down that spoon. Guess what? RPE doesn't work.

Here's a myth that fitness professionals have bought into big time, probably because people always think it's simpler to go with the subjective analysis of feelings rather than determine the facts. (This may have been true before the advent of the heart rate monitor, but definitely isn't true anymore!) After all, if you're in touch with your feelings, why bother collecting the data which could show it differently?

The problem is just this - perceived exertion using only your personal perceptions of effort to set your training intensities misses the target. It was quantified by exercise scientist Dr. Gunnar Borg in 1973 when he first based a rating scale on perceived exertion. For a sample of the problems with this paradigm, let me give an example of one of my workouts based on RPE.

I love to train with my dog Allez-Allez. She is a nine-year-old Queensland Healer and has her own training style - go hard all of the time, and chase a rabbit if you can. While I usually forego the rabbits, we love to run off-trail for hours. Sometimes, even I - a crown princess of heart rates - throw my heart rate monitor to the wind and just run, using my perceived exertion rating.

I know from years of cardiac monitor training that I get the greatest feeling of well-being running long distances, at sea level, on the flats (that is the description of every workout in my hometown of Sacramento, California), in my favourite easy and narrow heart rate zone of 150-155 bpm, or 77%-80% of my true Max HR. I've done these runs for years, so I should know how that rate feels... shouldn't I?

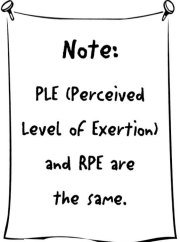

Note:

PLE (Perceived Level of Exertion) and RPE are the same.

I decided one day to test my theory, so I put on my Vantage XL monitor and took off with Allez-Allez for a 12-miler. This time, I put masking tape over the face of the watch so I wouldn't peek at my heart rate. I ran totally subjectively, chasing rabbits in my head, using my perception that I was running at my preferred exertion rate of the low 150s.

Immediately afterwards, I downloaded the information from my monitor into my computer, and to my consternation - but not great surprise - I found that I had done a steady state run at around 140 bpm. Basically, going by RPE left me feeling unhappy and dissatisfied.

Some researchers have found that perceived exertion can be very accurate. Others report it to be unacceptably inaccurate. It's my opinion that if you want to train with clear and accurate information, using the guess method attached to your feelings is probably not the most sound way. Remember Heart Zone Training principle #3: you manage best what you can measure and monitor.

HZT WITH RPE

There are some athletes who are addicted to their monitors. They wear them for every workout and then to work. There are times when it's fun to just go work out and not be conscious of intensity, percentages and zones. Take a break if you're an addict and feel your exertion freely.

THE EXTRA PARADIGM FOR HIGH-PERFORMANCE FOLKS

Most of my training friends know what their max VO_2 is.

Many know an inordinate amount of baseball trivia, too. The former is important to your training.

Often I read in one of the many popular sports and fitness magazines that a celebrity cyclist is training at a intensity of 85% VO_2 max for a 40K time-trial ride. How amusing. What does any of that mean to anyone who doesn't have a gas analyser on hand to calculate their oxygen uptake? It doesn't mean anything - it's physio-babble.

The other thing that always gnaws away at me in those same magazines is the suggested lactate threshold training levels. Do they think their readers have the ability to take their own blood samples while they're training, then pass the vials along to some handy lab they pass somewhere along their training course in order to have the lactate concentration analysed?

for your information:

VO_2 max means the maximum volume of oxygen you can utilise at any one moment. It's measured using a gas analyser and it changes dramatically with conditioning. A high VO_2 max is best because it means you can do a lot of work.

To a large extent these ludicrous recommendations are the fault of exercise scientists who are too fond of quoting exercise intensity in terms of their two favourite measurement tools: blood lactate and oxygen consumption. There is a cavernous gap in between them, with their labs chock full of hundreds of thousands of dollars of testing equipment, and us, armed only, if we're lucky, with our heart rate monitors.

The bottom line is that there are only three ways to measure your exercise intensity:

- Direct measurement of maximal oxygen consumption using analysis of expired air samples collected while the individual is exercising. Equipment cost: $10,000-$75,000 and retailers don't stock them.
- Blood samples taken during exercise and analysed for the concentration of lactic acid. Equipment cost: $500-$10,000, plus, a high messiness factor if attempted "on the run."
- Continuous measurement of heart rate with a personal heart rate monitor. Equipment cost: $75-$400.

Now, I am not trying to say that measuring oxygen uptake and lactates isn't worthwhile. Of course it is. These have been the measurement choices of exercise scientists for the last twenty-five years because they are the most accurate ways of measuring energy costs and training load. If you are at all serious about long-term fitness, I thoroughly recommend that at least once every ten years you have a complete physical, with lactates and oxygen consumption as part of the assessment, and that you keep these records and monitor your own aging process.

However, it seems clear to me, if not to those magazine editors, that it is only with a heart rate monitor that individuals can measure exercise training loads cheaply, accurately, practically, and on an ongoing basis.

Workout #3:
THE STEP-TRED-ROW-CYCLE HZT WORKOUT

My travel schedule has been hectic lately, plus I have had a debilitating Achilles tendon injury so I have sought a different protocol for exercising until both of those conditions change. I discovered a new one-hour indoor workout that I can do at the gyms in most hotels (which are usually these small rooms with four or five pieces of equipment) or at my athletic club which has kept me in great shape given the circumstances. It's a form of what's called indoor circuit training but it's done on machines rather than circuit stations and it's done by alternating zones. The circuit consists of four different machines, on each of which I do a three zone ladder. The sequence of the cardio circuit isn't key unless you want to vary between upper body and lower body equipment such as a stepper which is lower body and a rowing machine which is a lot of upper body. The sequence I particularly like is a stepper, a treadmill, a rowing machine and an exercise bike. I like to use three zones in the ladder - Z2 (60%-70% Max HR, Temperate Zone), Z3 (70%-80% Max HR, the Aerobic Zone), Z4 (80%-90% Max HR, the Threshold Zone) each for five minutes. Since I know those zones literally by heart now, I know how to solve the exercise machine problem - the exercise equipment sets the zone based on my age, they don't let me set the zones.

To overcome this problem, you have to "over-ride the formula," a formula that is preset in each piece of cardio equipment. Recovery phase of the workout is the time in between the four different machines and I use this time to answer all of its questions like "how much do you weigh," "what type of workout". I always have to override the formulas by saying I am 25 years old (actually I am 50) and I want to manually control the workout so I punch in that request.

I start each time in Z2 for the first five minutes and that allows me to comfortably warm the specific muscles that I am using on that machine as well as recover from the circuit before. For example, after I get off the stepper and start programming in my personal information into the treadmill, I am recovering from the stepper while I start walking at the floor of my Z2 zone which for me is 120 bpm. During that first five minutes, I slowly increase the belt speed so that I get to 130 bpm in about 2.5 minutes. This is the midpoint of my Z2 Temperate Zone and by the end of five minutes I have watched my heart rate increase to the ceiling of my Z2 which is the floor of my Z3 which is 145 bpm. I have to tell you that Z4, which is 80% of my Max HR, is the point that I can feel the intensity; and I hang out a lot in the lower half of my Z4 for that five minutes as it's hot in the upper half, or for me 170-180 bpm, for very long.

At the end of an hour, I feel that glow and good feeling that I get whenever I have a workout where I have maximised my time and gotten the most benefit possible. That's what this workout is all about - incredible cardiovascular benefit from every single minute of workout time.

Heart Rate Assessment

Before we go any further, you've probably got some questions. I'll bet the biggest one is, "How do I determine my Max HR?" That's the basis for all of Heart Zone Training, and that's what you need to do next.

Your maximum heart rate (Max HR) is a specific number, the maximum number of contractions per minute that your heart can make. There are a number of basic facts about Max HR that we need for reference:

- Max HR is genetically determined; in other words, you're born with it.
- Max HR is a fixed number, unless you become unfit.
- Max HR cannot be increased by training.
- Max HR declines with age only in sedentary individuals.
- Max HR is affected by drugs.
- Max HRs that are high do not predict better athletic performance.
- Max HRs that are low do not predict worse athletic performance.
- Max HR has great variability among people of the same age.
- Max HR for children has been measured at over 200 bpm.
- Max HR cannot be accurately predicted for most people by any mathematic formula.
- Max HR does not vary from day to day, but it is test-day sensitive.
- Max HR testing requires the person to be fully rested.
- Max HR testing needs to be done multiple times to determine the exact number.

For us, there's one more point to remember:

- **Max HR is the anchor point from which you set your individual heart training zones.**

Max HR is a critical piece of information, since you design your entire Heart Zone Training program around it. It serves as a marker for exercise intensity. There are a number of different approaches to capturing this number. These include taking a Max HR test to determine the true number or doing a SubMax test from which you can predict your Max HR pretty accurately.

♥ MAX HR GUIDELINES FOR DETERMINING MAX HR

The first step is to follow the guidelines that have been prescribed for exercise testing by the American College of Sports Medicine. Before taking any tests or following any exercise prescription, you should follow their prudent guidelines.

For more details refer to the *ACSM's Guidelines for Exercise Testing and Prescription,* Fifth ed., 1995.

Here, briefly, is a synopsis of the recommendations:

Apparently healthy men greater than age 40, and apparently healthy women greater than age 50, should have a medical examination and diagnostic exercise test before starting a vigorous exercise program, as should symptomatic men and women of any age. However, these procedures are not essential when such persons begin a moderate intensity exercise regimen.

If in doubt, prior to engaging in any vigorous physical activity or exercise test, consult your physician for clearance. It's wise to see your physician on a regular basis regardless, so get a clearance while you are there.

SUBMAX HR TESTS

If you aren't in shape and haven't been for awhile, you don't want to take a Max HR test designed to bring you to your actual maximum heart rate. Instead, there are best-guess methods which are much easier and accurate enough for you to use to begin training. These methods use sub-maximum testing to predict your Max HR. There is some error here, but these test/formula combos are better than just using the mathematical formulas alone, because they're specifically tailored to you.

Note: For the purposes of these tests, use the following definitions (these definitions refer to cardiovascular shape - not muscular):

Low Shape - if you do not exercise at all, or if you have not exercised recently (last 8 weeks). Remember, you can be thin, have no weight-loss goals, and still be in low shape.

Average Shape - you walk a mile 3 times a week, or participate in any aerobic activity 3 times a week for 20 minutes.

Excellent Shape - you regularly have training sessions that total more than 1 hour a week, or you walk or run at least 5 miles a week.

•THE SUBMAX 1-MILE WALKING TEST. Go to any high school or college track (most are 400 meters or 440 yards around) and walk or stride as fast as you can in your current condition. Walk or stride as fast as is comfortable in your current condition. Walk four laps which is equal to one mile.

The last lap is the important one. Take your pulse, or use your heart rate monitor, to determine your average heart rate for *only* the last lap. The first three laps are just to get you to reach a heart rate plateau and to stay there for the last lap.

Add to this average last lap heart rate one of the following that best matches your current fitness level:

1. **Low Shape:** +40 bpm
2. **Average Shape:** +50 bpm
3. **Excellent Shape:** +60 bpm

This final number (for example, an average 135 bpm last lap plus 60 bpm, because I'm in excellent shape, would equal 195 bpm for me) should be fairly close to your Max HR.

TAKING YOUR PULSE MANUALLY

Your heart rate and your pulse rate are usually, but not necessarily, equal. "Heart rate" refers to the electrical impulses that cause your heart to beat, but "pulse rate" refers only to the movement of blood through your arteries. If you have mitral fibrillation, you have no pulse rate but you have a heart rate. If you have cardiac arrest, you don't have a heart rate but you *do* have a pulse rate (for a short period of time, anyway).

Each time the left ventricle of the heart contracts, a surge of blood is pumped into the aorta and into the peripheral vessels of the arterial system. This stretch and subsequent recoil of the arterial wall during a complete cardiac cycle can be felt manually by applying light pressure over any artery that is near the surface of the skin. This stretch and recoil is what we usually are measuring when we talk about our "pulse."

To manually measure your radial pulse, take two fingers and place them over the inside surface of your wrist and lightly apply pressure. Wait quietly and move your fingers until you feel the blood flow. The reason that pulse is taken in the wrist is because it is safe and prominent. Other prominent locations are the groin and the neck (carotid pulse). However, taking your pulse rate from your neck's carotid artery can slow your heart rate and sometimes gives you a false reading.

Continued Next Page

Pulse can best be manually measured when you are stationary, which makes it a difficult method for determining training intensity for those who are exercising. When you stop exercising to count your pulse it almost immediately begins to drop - for some really fit people it plummets like a stone. This leads to calculating a pulse rate that is lower than what you are actually working at. It's common for those who are fit to see their pulse drop a beat per second. That can result in a 10-15 beat error when counting manually.

The easiest method is to count the number of pulse waves during six seconds and add a zero to that number to obtain the number of beats per minute. For example, in six seconds, if you count 8 beats then you add a zero and have the number 80 or eighty beats per minute. Others prefer to count pulse for ten seconds and multiply that number by six or for fifteen seconds and multiply times four. Accuracy of measurement is what's important here and sometimes it's difficult to multiply when you are tired, and your heart beating slows while you are counting, which is an additional reason why using a heart rate monitor is preferred.

• **THE SUBMAX STEP TEST.** Use an 8" step (almost any step in your home or in a club will do) and perform a 3-minute step test. After your warm-up, step up and down in a four-count sequence as follows: right foot up, left up, right down, left down. Each time you move a foot up or down, it counts as one step. Count "up, up, down, down" for one set, with 20 sets to the minute. It is very important that you don't speed up the pace - keep it regular.

After 2 minutes, you'll need to monitor your heart rate for the last minute. The SubMax Step Test now can be used to predict your Max HR. Add to your last minute's heart rate average one of the following numbers:

1. **Low Shape:** +55 bpm
2. **Average Shape:** +65 bpm
3. **Excellent Shape:** +75 bpm

Your result should be pretty close to your Max HR. (Again, my last-minute heart rate average might be something like 120 bpm, to which I'd add 75 bpm, bringing the total to 195 bpm.)

♥ MAX/HR MAX HEART RATE TESTS

There are a lot of ways to determine your Max HR and, of course, the least-risky method is to have your physician supervise your test. If a physician does this, also ask for a ventilatory threshold or anaerobic threshold test at the same time so you can have an accurate value for your anaerobic threshold heart rate as well (more on this later). You can also take a supervised graded stress test (GSX) at a sports laboratory. Call your local sports club for a referral.

Many fitness testing facilities offer sub-maximal exercise tests designed to bring you to 75-85% of your age-determined Max HR. The usefulness of these SubMax tests is questionable. Besides comparing your results to tables that suggest how "fit" you are based on your chronological, not biological age, their basic value is in recording your current exercise training load and corresponding heart rate in hopes that you will re-test and see changes. (This might be helpful, but you'll very probably know you are getting fitter without it). Some testing facilities will say they are taking you to your Max HR, but really they will only take you to your age-predicted Max HR (calculated as 220-age). This test is not what you want because it doesn't give you your "true" Max HR, just the mathematical one. Make sure you know what they are going to do in advance or request (maybe demand) a true Max HR test.

If you want an adequate test and exercise screening, invest in a Max HR test performed by an Exercise Test Technologist, certified by the ACSM, at a qualified facility. There is a broad range of fees and types of tests but the normal range for just a Max HR test is $75-$150US (or less if you are a student). Add another $100-$300US for a blood workup and VO_2 max test. Many times, your health insurance will cover some or all of these costs. By taking these tests, you are also able to keep a record of your fitness levels and changes as you age. It's advisable to take these tests every five years and compare the results over that time. This practice is good, sound preventive medicine because you take responsibility for measuring and monitoring your aging process.

An alternative is to take one of the self-administered Max HR tests described below - if you are apparently healthy and have no risks for cardiovascular or other diseases and meet the ACSM Guidelines outlined above - the fun begins.

• **2–4 MINUTE TEST.** This is a protocol that we have developed and refined that requires (without warm-up and warm-down time) between 2 and 4 minutes to complete. The test is best taken on a track, and it requires a partner who can run/bike with you throughout the test, to give heart rate readings aloud and set the pace. The runner being tested wears the chest transmitter belt and the partner wears the wrist monitor.

Start the test with an easy warm-up of at least 5 minutes or 2 laps. Your goal during the warm-up is to get your heart beating to 100-120 bpm (or to an estimated 60% of your Max HR). Without stopping, begin the test by gradually accelerating your speed so that your heart rate climbs about 5 bpm every 15 seconds. At each 15-second interval, your partner should tell you the exercise time and your heart rate and offer encouragement as he or she gradually, very gradually pushes you faster.

Within a 2- to 4-minute period, if your partner has set the pace correctly, your heart rate will cease to climb even with increased effort and pace. You'll know you are there when you can no longer accelerate and you hear your partner repeating the same number. At this point you've reached your Max HR and either you or your partner can call an end to the test. For detail description of the 2-4 minute test, go to Workout #4 in this chapter.

• **5K RACE TEST.** This can be taken by anyone skiing, running, biking, or snowshoeing. Enter a 5K race, and during the last 1–2 minutes go to a full sprint. Keep checking your heart rate monitor and add 5 beats to the highest number recorded there during this period. The result should be your Max HR (because of muscle fatigue, you can't drive yourself all the way to true Max HR at this point).

• BIGGEST NUMBER TEST. This is one of those that is simply obvious. Given that you've worn your heart rate monitor a while, especially during hard workouts, your Max HR is the biggest number you have ever seen on your heart rate monitor (the biggest *reasonable* number, not 300 bpm, say - you don't want to take one that's influenced by interference).

AMBIENT HEART RATE

It's not as critical to Heart Zone Training as the Max HR, but it is still of value to know your average daily heart rate - your "ambient" heart rate, also known as "sitting heart rate." This number, usually found when in a sitting position like behind a computer or in front of a television, normally varies little from day to day. When it does vary, especially if it goes up, it is a good indicator of your body being under some sort of stress. For example, you could be fatigued, overtrained, under mental or emotional stress (which is reflected in your body by physical stress), your immune system lowered by an oncoming cold, etc. The lower your ambient heart rate the better. This is a *trainable* and *moveable* number that decreases with fitness and increases with inactivity.

Raising your heart rate does not make you fit. You can raise your heart rate by thinking.

To determine your ambient heart rate, take your pulse or wear your heart monitor and jot down in your calendar or day planner sitting heart rate numbers that you see or count throughout the day, perhaps for several days over a week. The average number will be your ambient heart rate.

RECOVERY HEART RATE.

One of the best indicators of fitness is to take a recovery heart rate assessment. There are a variety of recovery heart rate tests, but one of the most popular is the "120 second" test. The purpose of the test is to measure how quickly you recover back toward your ambient heart rate. The faster the better; the fitter you are. If you recover quickly, it means that your ability to restore oxygen and nutrients to the muscles is more efficient.

Select a steady state heart rate number like the midpoint of Z3. My Z3 range is 140-160 bpm and my midpoint is 150 bpm. Exercise for a period of time say 15 minutes at your steady state midpoint after an adequate warm-up. Stop the exercise and stand or sit in a relaxed position. Measure the change in heart rate. For example, it's common to see in a fit person heart rates drop as much as one beat per second for the first minute. In two minutes, it's not uncommon to see a 60-70 beat decrease in heart rate.

A recovery heart rate formula is as follows:

150 bpm	–	90 bpm	=	60 bpm
Exercise heart rate		rate at end of 120 seconds		Recovery heart rate (difference)

If you prefer a shorter elapsed time say sixty seconds, you'll see a quicker drop in heart rate.

There are other recovery heart rate assessments. Recovery heart rate is a measurement commonly used during interval training. Select a recovery heart rate number such as the floor of Z 2 as your take-off point and the floor of Z5 as your highest intensity allowable interval number.

Recovery heart rate is a tool in your training arsenal to provide you with information you wouldn't otherwise have. Most interval workouts use recovery *time* or *distance* not recovery heart rate as the method for determining when to begin the next interval cycle. Time may or may not allow you adequate recovery because it can't rely on your physiological response to your current status. If you are in an overtrained or fatigued condition, you'll need more time to recover adequately which heart rate recovery can measure - your stopwatch simply can't know this.

DELTA HEART RATE

By definition, your Delta heart rate is the difference between your standing and prone or lying down heart rate numbers. Some exercise scientists call this the orthostatic test. Whenever you stand, you are changing the training load on the cardiac system requiring the heart to pump blood against the forces of gravity. A low Delta heart rate number demonstrates that your heart can adjust to change efficiently. A higher Delta heart rate number means you are not as fit cardiovascularly and may well be an indicator of increased stress from either internal or external conditions.

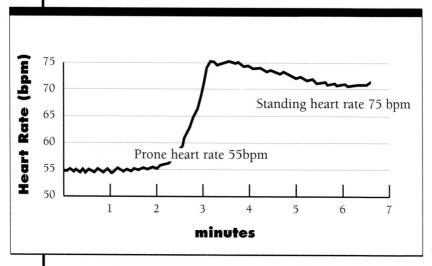

Standing heart rate 75 bpm

Prone heart rate 55bpm

Here's how to take a Delta self test:

Lie down on your back in a resting, quiet state for two minutes. Note your heart rate in this prone position. Slowly, stand upright and note your increased heart rate and record it every 15 seconds until it levels off. The difference between these two numbers - standing minus prone - is your Delta heart rate. The following graph shows a Delta heart rate of 20 beat or difference between standing heart rate of 75 bpm minus the prone position heart rate of 55 bpm.

RESTING HEART RATE

Two heart rate numbers are frequently confused: resting and ambient. Resting heart rate is that count taken in bed before you rise. It is your pre- rolling over and hugging, getting up to use the bathroom heart rate. Your resting heart rate is found when you *first* open your eyes in the morning.

Your heart rate changes with the time of day, increasing during the daylight hours and decreasing during the night time.

Resting heart rate is one of the key signals or markers for athletes of overtraining or other conditions that might be arising. The five-beat rule applies here: if your resting heart rate is five bpm above normal, you should train only in the low-intensity zones or take the day off.

It's clear that these two heart rate numbers - ambient and resting - drop with training. This is called the "Training Effect." Because of this training effect you save an incredible number of heartbeats in your lifetime. Critics can scoff at fitness freaks who love to push their hearts into their upper zones, but over a lifetime, it's a bargain.

Fitness has a cumulative effect. It pays off in the short term and in the long run. In this case, the person who has been working out for their adult life can save over 400 million contractions of their heart muscle. It's your choice. Fitness pays for itself.

Workout #4:
TESTING YOUR MAX HR

Because the accurate assessment of your Max HR is crucial to the development of any effective training or fitness program, most coaches and trainers advocate verifying estimates with actual performance tests. These tests can be conducted by exercise technologists and other health professionals in a laboratory setting or self-administered.

A word of caution to all of our readers. Do not take self-administered tests if you are over 35 years of age, have been sedentary, or for any reason are in poor physical condition and have not had a thorough physical exam (including an exercise stress test) and a physician's release.

The American College of Sports Medicine also offers the following warning: At or above 35 years of age, it is necessary

HOW DO YOU SAVE 473,040,000 HEARTBEATS?

Ambient Heartbeat	Unfit Person	Fit Person
Beats Per Minute	70*	50
Beats in a Day	100,800	72,000
Beats in a Year	36,792,000	26,280,000
Total Beats in 45 Years	1,655,640,000	1,182,600,000

Difference: 473,040,000 heartbeats

* Average daily rate including ambient heart rate and resting heart rates.

for individuals to have a medical examination and a maximal exercise test before beginning a vigorous exercise program. At any age, the information gathered from an exercise test may be useful to establish an effective and safe exercise prescription. Maximal testing done for men at age 40 or above or women age 50 and older, even when no symptoms or risk factors are present should be performed with physician supervision.

You should also know that the American College of Cardiology and the American Heart Association question the value of diagnostic exercise testing in apparently healthy individuals.

Talk to your own personal physician to determine what Max HR calculation or test is appropriate for you.

A maximal stress test and health appraisal by a physician or sports physiologist is the safest and most recommended way to determine your precise Max HR. The test is usually administered on a treadmill or exercise bicycle and it simulates increased training load by increasing the pace, resistance or the surface incline.

During the test you will be forced to exercise extremely hard. The test will continue until an increased intensity of exercise does not cause an increase in heart rate. At that point, you've reached your max.

It is only natural that the test will create some muscular pain and you will feel very uncomfortable. But, if breathing difficulties or any pains occur, especially in the chest, the test should be terminated immediately.

There are a number of tests you can take to verify your Max HR calculation. In my book, *Heart Zone Training*, I have included several of them.

To insure a more accurate Max HR reading, I have developed a refined protocol which requires only two to four minutes of hard

effort. Please keep in mind, the maximal stress test cautions mentioned previously also apply to self-administered tests.

Before and after taking any Max HR test, or just exercising for that matter, you should warm up and cool down. How long and how hard is an individual choice. Remember, the purpose is to ease your body from a resting state to an active once and back again.

Just like any other muscle, the heart needs to warm up before going all out and to slow down before coming to an abrupt stop.

The Two-to-Four-Minute Max HR test can be best performed on a track and it requires a partner who can run with you throughout the test, give HR readings and set a hard pace. The runner being tested wears the chest transmitter belt while the partner wears the wrist monitor.

Start the test with an easy warm-up of at least five minutes or two laps. Your goal during the warm-up is to get your heart working at about 110-130 beats per minute or about 60 percent of your age estimated Max HR.

After warming up, and without stopping, gradually accelerate your speed so that your heart rate climbs about five beats every 15 seconds. At 15-second intervals, your partner should tell you the time and your heart rate and offer on-going encouragement to gradually push harder.

Within a two to four-minute window, if your partner sets the pace correctly, your heart rate will cease to climb even with increased effort and pace. At that point, you've reached your max and your partner should call an end to the test or you simply won't be able to run another step! A diagram of your test might look like the above chart.

During that last 15-30 seconds of the test as you continue to gradually accelerate, your partner should keep repeating your heart rate over and over. Eventually, the same number will be repeated because your heart won't go higher - it's a finite number.

TRAINING ZONES

After completing a medically appropriate performance test and determining your Max HR, you are ready to develop a training or fitness program around a training zone which meets your current level of fitness and goals. Get out your calculator or pencil and compute your five training zones.

RUNNING MAX HEART RATE TEST

Equipment

- Testee w/chest transmitter
- Partner Testor w/receiver watch and stopwatch
- 400 meter track, running gear
- Optional: an extra monitor for Testee to wear

Steps

1. Warm-up w/2-6 easy laps at 60 percent of mathematically-calculated Max HR.
2. At starting point, partner sets gradually increasing pace. The goal is to reach the max between two and four minutes.
3. Every 15 seconds partner gives HR and elapsed time such as "One minute, 155."
4. If you reach the 3 minute mark, continue to accelerate but you need to reach max within the next 60 seconds
5. By the end, you are running extremely fast, can no longer talk and are breathing rapidly and hard.
6. Partner should now be repeating loudly Testee's HR every 5

seconds yelling positively and gradually accelerating until you can no longer maintain form, speed or willingness to run. You've max'd when HR no longer climbs. Partner calls the end to the test. Warm down slowly and actively.

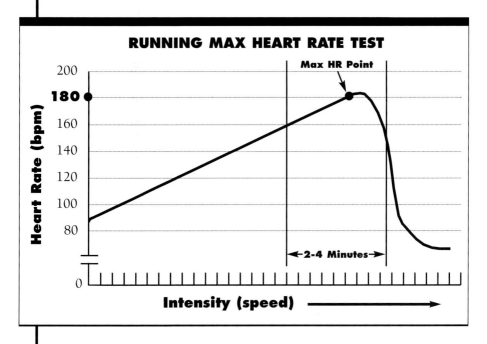

The Five Heart Training Zones

Are you on the bus yet? I hope you're in the midst of throwing off the paradigms that were weighing you down and are planning to take a test or two to calculate your maximum heart rate. Now you've come to the good stuff, the "heart" of the matter, so to speak! In this chapter, we're going to introduce you to the basic details you'll need to individualise and maximise your training.

Heart Zone Training is designed around a framework of progressively more challenging heart rate "zones." These zones are based on percentages of each person's Max HR, so Heart Zone Training is actually a doubly individualised system. (That's why it works so reliably and efficiently!). You set your training zones based on your Max HR, and then you choose the zone(s) you want to train in based on your goals at any given time.

Each heart rate training zone covers a ten-percent range of your Max HR. As the zones change, so do the metabolic and physiological events; fuel utilisation changes (your body burns fats most efficiently in one zone over another, for example), lactates and oxygen utilisation changes (you can train aerobically or anaerobically), metabolic activity changes (you can train toward your goal of faster competitive performance or having a healthier heart), and most importantly of all, *you* change. Meeting and exceeding your fitness goals is the true pleasure of Heart Zone Training.

It's easy to follow the Heart Zone Training system because it's *your* individualised prescription; it's your plan; it's your body; it's under your control. Not only are you on the bus, you're the driver.

Whichever way you choose to do it, once you start to monitor your heart rate you can watch yourself reach your goals - whether you want to lose weight or fat, gain muscle, body sculpt, get fitter, get healthier, improve your heart, or expand your mind drug-free. It's powerful. Competitive athletes say it's a weapon. For any of us, whatever our goals, it's definitely an advantage. Welcome to a system that's so well-suited to *you* it can't help but work!

ALL ABOUT ZONES

There are some special characteristics of Heart Zone Training zones that make them what they are. Keep 'em in mind as we make our way through the following chapters.

1. Zones have size. The size of each zone is a 10% range of your true Max HR. The size of the zone in number of beats depends on how high your true Max HR is. Given a 200 bpm Max HR (which is very convenient for multiplying), each of the five zones would be 10% of 200, or 20 beats wide. Most zones for most people range from 15 to 20 beats in size; this is big enough to allow for some "wiggle room" when you are working out, but small enough to be on target for your particular training goal(s).

2. Zones have structure. A zone may be viewed as being made up of two different parts: its top and bottom halves. In other words, inside every zone is an upper and a lower zone. So, while the whole Aerobic zone may be from 70% to 80% of your Max HR, the lower half of the zone is 70%-75% (or 140-150 bpm in our 200 bpm Max HR example), and the upper Aerobic zone is 75%-80% (or 150-160 bpm in this case). It's just a way to subdivide a medium-sized heart window into two smaller, even more focused parts.

3. Zones have dividing lines. The upper and lower limits of each zone coincide with the floor and ceiling of its bordering zones. The floor of the Z3 Aerobic zone, for example, is 70% of your Max HR. This floor, or threshold, is that heart rate where you first break into this zone. Seventy percent of your Max HR also happens to be where the Temperate zone ends. The Aerobic zone ceiling, 80% Max HR, is the line at the very top of the zone. At this point you are passing through the Aerobic zone ceiling into the floor of the next higher and more intense zone, the anaerobic Threshold zone.

4. Zone names correspond with their benefits.
Each heart rate zone has a specific benefit that comes from the physiological activities that happen when you exercise within that zone. For example, the Z1 Healthy Heart zone is exactly that, the range of heart rates where most individuals realise the most cardiovascular benefits, leading to improved heart and lung function.

5. Zones have numbers.
There are certain specific and measurable events that are so exact that they're represented by a single heartbeat value called a heart rate number. We've talked about a few of them: the maximum heart rate number and resting heart rate number are specific heart rate numbers that are located in relationship to (inside or on the dividing lines of) the zones. For example, the diagram below is the location of your Max HR on the ceiling of Zone 5.

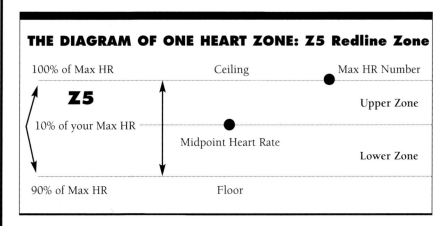

THE DIAGRAM OF ONE HEART ZONE: Z5 Redline Zone

100% of Max HR — Ceiling — Max HR Number

Z5 — Upper Zone

10% of your Max HR — Midpoint Heart Rate — Lower Zone

90% of Max HR — Floor

6. Zones are a subset of the wellness continuum.
The wellness continuum consists of three areas of physical well-being - health, fitness, and performance - and we need to keep in mind that we're not all going to have our goals in the same areas. This is why your friend, who's a veteran marathoner, might complain about what kind of "shape" he or she is in, while you would kill to look the way they do and be so fit and healthy. The health area covers those training zones that promote health but don't primarily improve physical fitness and certainly not performance. To measure improvements in health, we seek positive changes in blood pressure, body fat, cholesterol, etc. To measure improvements in fitness, however, its positive changes in oxygen utilisation, lactate concentrations and heart rate numbers we're looking for. And, to measure improvements in performance, positive changes in completion times, accuracy of movement skill, mental attitude, lactate threshold, and other indices are used.

7. Zones use time, not distance, as their measurement tool. That is, the amount of time you spend in each zone is the way you measure your workout, not in miles run or the number of strokes per minute cycled or rowed. This measurement is called "time in zone" and is measured in the number of minutes that you spend in each zone. For example, one day you decide to run for 30 minutes in the Aerobic zone; the following day you might choose to walk for 50 minutes in your Temperate zone. Varying your workouts, both in activity and zone, allows you to get multiple benefits from your training.

8. Zones have specific numerical values. When we talk about "exercise by the numbers," that means doing workouts based on the specific numbers that make up your exact zones. For example, if your true, tested Max HR is 200 beats per minute and you wanted a high fat-burning day as a percent of your fuels burned, you would calibrate that workout to be in Z1-Z3. If you really wanted to fine-tune your training, you might choose to narrow the heart window to Z3. Use the chart on page 66 to determine the specific numerical values for your five zones.

9. Higher zones require less time in zone than lower zones. You can train at the lower zones, or "cruise" zones, as they are sometimes called, for longer periods of time than in the higher zones. As you move up to higher intensity zones, you need to decrease the amount of time that you spend in that zone, particularly in the top two, the anaerobic Threshold and Redline zones. This simply makes sense; you can walk farther than you can sprint, and overdoing it is nearly a guarantee of injuries or burnout.

10. Zones are relative. Your five heart rate zones are specific to *your* maximum heart rate, not anybody else's. With two runners, each maintaining a heart rate of 160 bpm, one might well be in their Z4 Threshold Zone and the other may be in their Z2 Temperate Zone. It's all relative.

11. Zones help to quantify workload. You may have heard of the expression "get fit by using F.I.T.". Those three letters together and with a little math can become a way to quantify training load or the total quantity of exercise you experience. This is called exercise dosage, too. The letter "F" means frequency or how often do you train say in a week. The letter "I" stands for intensity which you now know means which of five heart zones or what percent of your max HR. The letter "T" is for time and it is usually measured in minutes as in how long or how many minutes you should exercise.

> You can skip ahead to Chapter 12 if you want to read about quantifying exercise frequency, intensity, and time into the HZT Point System.

12. Zones are a state of mind. The Japanese businessmen whom I mentioned earlier taught me that when they explained the level of physical fitness in their country. Remember *watch-do-be*?

I asked them during the middle of the meeting, which was very American of me, which of the three stages in the watch-do-be progression they personally were in at that time. It was one of those let's-go-around-the-table confessions, and the guilt and absolution flowed like saki.

Each started by explaining that their lives were out of balance, that they worked too much, and that they didn't prioritise what was truly important to them. They said they had come to realise that their health and their families were more important than their business status and the yen in their bank accounts. It was as if it were the first time (and maybe it was) they had acknowledged it to each other, that there was, in fact, a personal mission to their business mission to California. All four of them agreed that they were former "watchers" that had developed into "doers," and that this was part of both a cultural and personal transformation for them. But you could tell they wanted to know how to take that final step towards the pinnacle of the pagoda of mental-physical-emotional balance, of personal integrated fitness - they wanted to *be*.

I told them their goal of "being" healthy, of "being" fit was an attitude, a state of mind. It was all in their head. It was all in their muscles. It was all in their soul. But it could be experienced by connecting the body and the *heart,* with the head through the process of Heart Zone Training.

Zone		Frequency	Intensity	Time	Activity
Red Line	**Z5**	0-2 times/week	90-100%	2-4 min.	Racing, intervals, speed work
Threshold	**Z4**	1-3 times/week	80-90%	15-55 min.	Run, spinning, cc skiing
Aerobic	**Z3**	4-6 times/week	70-80%	20 min-2 hrs.	Jog, swim, cycle, step
Temperate	**Z2**	3-4 times/week	60-70%	15-30 min.	Jog/walk, swim, cycle
Healthy Heart	**Z1**	2-3 times/week	50-60%	10-60 min.	Walk, low-impact aerobics

run • bike • swim • hike • cycle • step • ski • jog • walk • race • spin

AN OVERVIEW OF THE FIVE ZONES:
THE GRADED STRESS TEST

While you wouldn't normally pass through each of the five zones in a single workout, there is one situation where this happens - what physicians call a graded stress test. The graded stress test is great for accurately setting each of your heart rate zones, but in this case it is also very useful for giving us an overview of what each of the zones are about.

Throughout the test, measurements of the amount of oxygen you consume and the amount of carbon dioxide you expire are tracked. At the same time, the physician might also be taking small amounts of blood to measure your blood concentration of lactate, a byproduct of energy metabolism. In addition, your heart rate is continuously measured by a cardiovascular monitoring system.

You start by stretching and warming up, and then you slowly begin to exercise either on a bike or, in our example, on a treadmill. Progressively, the speed of the treadmill periodically increases, and as the intensity changes, your heart rate increases.

The first thing that you'll notice is a time lag between the start of exercise and the heart, respiratory and blood responses. This is because it takes a minute or two for your heart to gear up to the body's demand. Look at the chart on page 70 and note that between A and B there's a lag between supply and demand.

Very soon the appropriate responses occur; the body catches up and gets the message that exercise has begun. This is called "the second-wind phenomenon." To you, it'll feel like the exercise has become easier, when in fact you've just caught up with the jump in metabolic demand from the beginning of the workout. This slow coming up to speed occurs most often in Z2.

As the intensity increases, you pass into the Temperate zone. Here you're in a fairly balanced metabolic state, but the pace is still quickening. During this period, there's a steady increase in oxygen uptake, blood circulation, and your body's fuel requirements; and the fuel mixture is beginning to change more to carbohydrates.

As the pace continues to increase, the aerobic floor is crossed. Carbon dioxide continues to be excreted through the lungs and doesn't yet start to accumulate in the muscle tissues. Almost all of the lactic acid produced is metabolised or converted back to glucose by other tissues, so it's also not accumulating. As you pass into the upper Aerobic zone, your fuel mix changes from predominantly fat burning to a state where more carbohydrates are required for fuel.

Eventually, as you pass through the Z3 Aerobic Zone ceiling, you enter the anaerobic Threshold. Aerobic ("with oxygen") metabolism can no longer provide the additional energy required to handle this training load or speed, and the proportion of fats burned is lower in the total energy mix. At these intensities, your muscles start to produce lactates faster than your body can dispose or "resynthesize" them. At this same heart rate number there's a change in respiratory function as well. Breathing becomes noticeably harder. This change in breathing pattern is often referred to as the ventilatory threshold. But you haven't yet reached your max: as the treadmill goes faster, you can still run faster. You've passed through your anaerobic or ventilatory threshold.

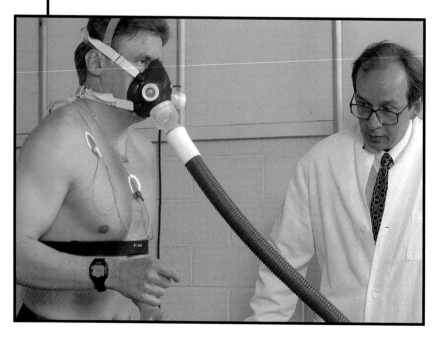

As you pass into the Z5 Redline zone, you reach the VO_2 max point where you can continue to run faster, but you can no longer increase the amount of oxygen that you are consuming. Right now, you will need encouragement to continue, because you will want to quit. But you can still run faster, and your heart rate continues to increase. After this point, the longest you can run on the treadmill, if you are *super* fit, is a matter of a few minutes - be prepared for the end to come soon. From here on the test requires that you have the internal and external motivation to continue to run so you can reach your Max HR. You're burning almost pure glucose for fuel, and your time is running short - less than a minute. Your lactates are rising exponentially, and within moments you must stop, absolutely exhausted. All you can hear is your breathing, which is at a maximum, your legs are wobbling from fatigue, your heart is pounding in your chest, you might be experiencing confusion and you feel this sense of happiness (or nausea) - because the stress test is over.

The treadmill speed drops quickly, and you slow your pace to an easy jog-walk for a cool-down. As you are recovering, you drop back through each of the zones as your heart rate drops and oxygen and metabolic demands once again can be easily met. Now you have the data that you need to determine your heart rate points and to set your zones. Oh yes, and it was a little painful as well - exercising to your max anything is always that way.

A final caveat, this standard graded stress test tends to predict a Max HR 3-10 beats below your true Max. This is because of the length of time that the test requires - sometimes as long as 20 minutes for performance athletes. During such a long testing time, the fatigue is so great in your leg muscles that your heart doesn't reach its Max HR. Take the 2-4 minute Max HR test described in Chapter 4 to assess more accurately for true Max HR.

THE GRADED STRESS TEST

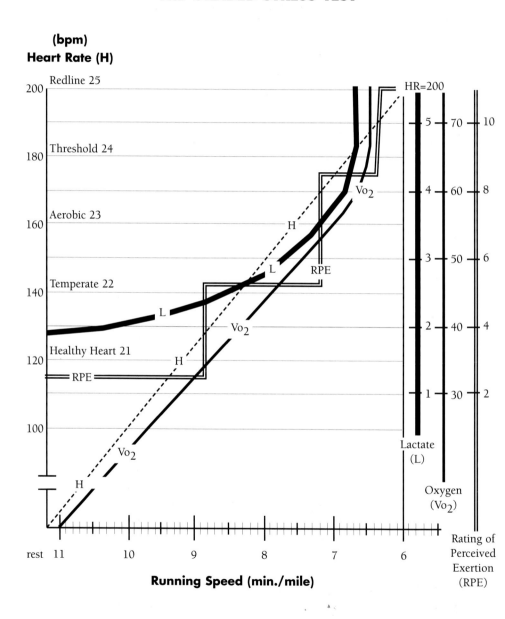

Workout #5:
X-C SKIING INTERVAL WORKOUT

Introduction. We all owe a debt of thanks to the cross country skiers. They were first to rapidly endorse heart training and help launch the revolution of higher performance conditioning using heart rate (HR) monitors. As the colds of winter transition us to cross country skiing and sport snowshoeing season, here's one of my favourite "in-season" workouts. Being a total body sport, cross country skiing puts as much demand and burn on the chest and breathing muscles as on the legs, arms, and mind-body.

Purpose. Intervals are key to nordic skiing because they simulate racing at high heart rates on the uphills and active recovery on the downhills. A cross country ski race is a series of intervals, so this workout is race specific training.

Workout Preparation. Find a loop course that will take about five minutes to complete. It should be reasonably flat, well-groomed, and secluded from heavy recreational ski traffic. Your max HR is sport specific. As a result, remember to test it for each different sport.

Workout Plan. This workout is a set of 5-10 loops with a three minute active rest between loops.

Workout. Warm up with one or two loops at 60-70 percent of Max HR. For the first two loops, ski at the top of Zone 3 (80 percent Max HR), then ski the last three loops at the top of the midpoint of Zone 4 (85 percent). Include three minutes of active rest between each loop. (That's a 2:1 work to rest ratio). Warm down by skiing one loop at no more than 60 percent Max HR. Time yourself during this workout and write it in your log along with your HR averages.

Frequency. Do this training session once each week. Increase the number of loops per session to 10 by the time you are peaking for your most important race.

Helpful Hints

- Don't be concerned about your HR during the first 60 seconds of your loops. Because of the "softening of the algorithms" or the way the HR monitor calculates, it will take about a minute to match your actual HR.

- Don't sacrifice technique for top heart rates. If your technique begins to suffer, step back in your interval training and work on longer intervals with more emphasis on technique than speed.

- Share your interval sessions with a friend. Match yourself with someone whose times and HR percentages are close to yours so you can encourage and "hammer" each other together. It will make you both better athletes.

The Z1 Healthy Heart Zone

The search has been on for the fountain of youth since before poor Ponce de Leon ever set foot on Florida soil, but it's beginning to look like our goal is in sight. Ponce, a Spanish explorer who arrived in the new world in the 1500's, may have died from the blood-thirsty mosquitoes, but many now are dying from the effects of obesity and sedentarism. The truth is that those deaths today are as needless as Ponce's was.

There's still no miracle cure, unless common sense and sound physiology have become miraculous, but there is a clear route to well-being and life extension: the Healthy Heart zone. Your body doesn't *have* to decline with age; we *choose* to send ourselves into a physical free-fall simply by becoming less active as we get older, triggering an ever-accelerating downward spiral. If you're in one of those spirals, turn your nose upward, look up at the sky and start to soar back up. Entering the Healthy Heart zone is your first step. Here you'll begin a workout program that guides you to the fountain of youth by breaking through the cardiovascular floor - 50% of your Max HR.

QUALITY OVER QUANTITY

As fitness expert Covert Bailey says, it's muscles that make the tiger sleek and let the eagle soar. Well, you'll find your wings in the Healthy Heart zone - it's the launching pad of the wellness continuum. It is probably the most important zone of all because it's the first point where the health benefits of exercise are realised.

Being at the easiest, most comfortable intensity range - 50%-60% Max HR - the Healthy Heart zone has taken some hard knocks from many fitness professionals. For years, many have said that there's simply no benefit to exercising in this zone, because there is no improvement in the body's oxygen utilisation. However, there *is* noticeable improvement in several other wellness categories: blood pressure lowers, cholesterol levels improve, body fat decreases or stabilises, and muscle mass increases.

> **If you walk 2 miles a day in 30 minutes, 3 times a week, death from all causes is reduced by 55%.**
>
> ~ Ken Cooper, M.D.

These are the reasons to work out in the Healthy Heart zone - because you want to get healthier. If your goal is to be a competitive athlete, you will probably only spend time warming up and warming down in this zone. If your interests are to improve your health, especially if you are just starting a fitness program, the Healthy Heart zone is the place to be.

The zone floor for the Healthy Heart zone is 50% of your Max HR. When you cross this heart rate line, you will realize health benefits. The amount of energy burned during this time will not be as great as in higher zones, but you will be burning a relatively large percentage of the *type* of calories that are most preferred as your source of fuel - fat. There's a critical, but not well discussed difference between total calories burned and the type of calories burned. Quality, or type of calories burned, is generally more important than quantity, the total number of calories expended in a workout. In the Healthy Heart zone, while the total calories burned per workout may be low, a very large percentage of the calories are fat calories. Carbohydrates are high-grade fuels, perfect for burning in the higher training load training zones. But burning them up doesn't slim you down, it might just make you hungrier!

The Healthy Heart zone is a very comfortable level of exercise - you get the feeling that you could go on forever. The average number of calories burned per minute (about 6) is lower than in any other zone, though. So, if your number one goal is not basic cardiovascular fitness, but fat loss, you'll need to move up to the Temperate zone, Zone 2.

Even if you have more advanced goals, the Z1 Healthy Heart zone is a good place to start, as well as to come back to from time to time, when you need a break from more strenuous workouts. Here you'll find the quiet kind of success that sticks with you; you'll feel good about yourself, you won't sweat profusely, and you'll be going at a moderate enough pace to have time to actually enjoy both the scenery and the workout.

Zone	Zone Name	% Max HR	Fuels Burned	Calories
Z1	Healthy Heart	50%–60%	10% Carbohydrates 60%-85% Fat 5% Protein	±5 calories per minute

IS P.E. P.C.? OR IS PHYSICAL EDUCATION POLITICALLY CORRECT?

Maybe you grew up with the experience of physical education that many of us did. PE teachers only had 30 minutes a day for you to actually experience the joy of exercise, so they worked you hard. At the beginning of the school year, you had to take a fitness test, and if you were like most people, you did poorly. That teacher with the whistle was trying to whip you into shape. What it probably did was whip you right out of physical fitness until now.

Mandatory physical education has been eliminated from many schools today, and you might be surprised to hear that I think this is a big mistake. Getting sufficient cardiovascular exercise every day is crucial to children's fitness, growth, and weight maintenance. With the number of obese children growing yearly, this is not a light matter. Many adults have lost their former, youthful fitness and are now struggling to regain it, but just imagine the immensity of your task if you were *never* fit, not even as a child!

I actually spent some time teaching physical education, and

when I did, I found the most crucial step was getting kids to enjoy themselves. Heck, many of the *teachers* struggled teaching PE because the class was about discipline, not about starting youngsters on the path of lifetime fitness. As far as any mention of heart rate zones went, the most physical education teachers were taught was to try to get kids into the target heart rate zone of 70%-85% Max HR, which is far above the Healthy Heart zone and many sedentary kids' abilities.

As adults, we have the luxury of choosing our own preferred forms of physical education, and we can also take advantage of the fact that we now know that working out in the Healthy Heart zone (50%–60% of your Max HR) is sufficient for great health benefits to occur. For those who have been inactive for more than five years, this is a perfect training load level with which to begin a program. If your Max HR were 200, it would mean that you would be spending your time in the 100-120 bpm zone.

The table below illustrates the Healthy Heart Zone ranges based upon 50% to 60% of specified Max HR.

Z1 Healthy Heart Zone 50% - 60% Maximum Heart Rate Chart

Max HR	150	155	160	165	170	175	180	185	190	195	200	205	210 bpm
50%	75	78	80	83	85	88	90	93	95	98	100	102	105
60%	90	93	95	99	102	105	108	111	114	117	120	123	125

GIVE A LITTLE, GET A LOT

The ACSM now acknowledges, after it re-reviewed the scientific literature, that working out in the Healthy Heart zone reduces your risk for certain degenerative diseases. (Remember- its 1990 exercise prescription "position stand" recommended from 60% to 90% Max HR as the training zone for workouts.)

The Healthy Heart zone doesn't fit this prescription because it is below the recommended 60%-90%. And that's the reason for the wellness continuum. Sure enough, if you want to *improve* fitness you will want to be in a higher zone, but if you want to get *healthier*, start out with the Healthy Heart zone.

When I give talks about Heart Zone Training, I often get two types of questions: What is the optimum exercise intensity and duration for a training workout? And, what is the minimum exercise intensity and duration for a training workout? With the Healthy Heart zone, you can get away with doing a little and still get an optimum benefit. It's the fitness version of having your cake and eating it, too!

The fact is, a little exercise makes a bigger health difference to you than a lot of exercise. That is, physical activity follows the law of diminishing returns - with more exercise you don't get a commensurate increase in benefits.

The figure below illustrates this phenomenon:

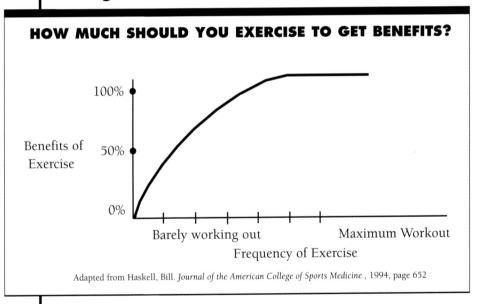

HOW MUCH SHOULD YOU EXERCISE TO GET BENEFITS?

Benefits of Exercise

100%

50%

0%

Barely working out   Maximum Workout

Frequency of Exercise

Adapted from Haskell, Bill. *Journal of the American College of Sports Medicine* , 1994, page 652

A little *can* be better than a lot. A lot of exercise may give you the maximum benefits, but not the optimum benefits. For example, Dr. Ken Cooper in this book, *Antioxident Revolution,* argues that excessive exercise constitutes a risk because of the release of "free radicals."

If you are working out for your health - to lower your risk of heart attacks, improve your immune system, lower your percentage of body fat - then exercising in the Healthy Heart zone will maximise your return on your fitness effort invested. Sure, there are additional benefits when you train in the four higher zones, but many of the benefits can already be achieved right here.

The greatest benefits happen to those who need them the most, the least active individuals who begin a low-intensity rate exercise program. They are going to see much greater health benefits than the marathon runner who adds another ten miles a week of running. Sure, the ten miles may produce some incremental speed or endurance benefit, but not the massive health improvements that you will see when a secretary or computer nerd moves out from behind their computer screen and gets into a low-intensity exercise program. The figure on the next page illustrates the point: A little exercise goes a long way towards gaining benefits.

If you've been relatively inactive and want to begin a fitness program, it's not only more efficient to work out in the Healthy Heart zone, it's also safer. This is the zone that has the least orthopedic or cardiac risk. Please don't be one of those stereotypical, gung-ho exercise fanatics who wants all of their results in the first week, because for better *and* worse, exercise is a double-edged sword. Training can either make you healthier and increase your resistance to disease or, if you overdo it, it can injure you and decrease your immune potential. And your risk is more related to the intensity of the exercise than its amount or frequency. It's better to exercise a little longer in the low-intensity zones than shorter periods at high-intensity levels. It's *not* true that the more pain, the more gain. For example, there is more of a risk of catching a cold, breaking bones, and heart attacks in the high heart rate zones than in the low ones. In other words, I don't recommend pushing yourself, because it's possible that you could fall.

It *is* true that with less pain there's more gain. In fact, *for some health benefits such as lowering blood pressure, reducing platelet aggregation and enhancing immune function, exercise in the three lower zones (the Healthy Heart, Temperate, and Aerobic zones) is more beneficial than exercise in the higher zones.*

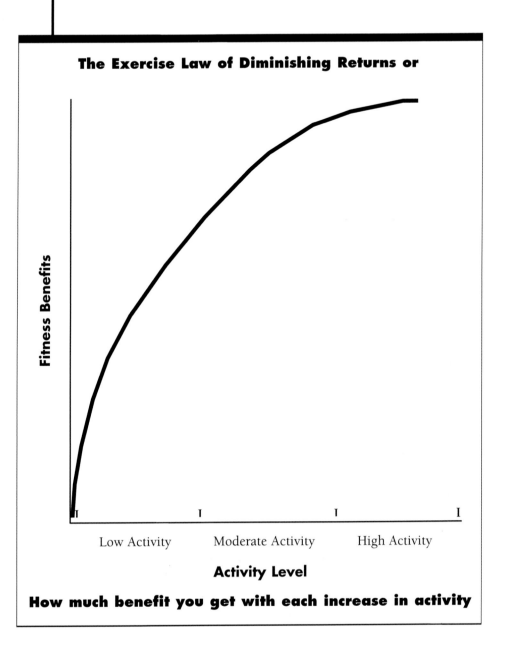

The Exercise Law of Diminishing Returns or

Fitness Benefits

Low Activity   Moderate Activity   High Activity

Activity Level

How much benefit you get with each increase in activity

TRAINING VOLUMES AND
THE PRINCIPLE OF EQUIVALENCY

Everybody wants an exercise program that gets them the most benefits in the least amount of time. You can have it with just two caveats: you've got to measure your heart rate (preferably, but not necessarily, with a heart rate monitor) and you must stay in the Healthy Heart zone the equivalent of 10 minutes a day. Quite simply, it doesn't matter whether you do 10 minutes a day or 20 minutes every other day. What matters is that you do it. After nearly a century of exercise testing, the answer to how much, how long, and how hard has been answered.

If you train 10 minutes a day, you will even be following the ACSM minimum workout guidelines of 20 minutes or longer, three times a week. That's a total exercise time of 60 minutes a week, and 60 minutes a week is the same to your body whether it's three times at 20 minutes each or six times at 10 minutes. The body doesn't care when you indulge in low intensity exercise – it only responds to exercise volume. Low intensity exercise can be accumulated in bits and pieces: twelve 5-minute periods or something equivalent is not better or worse than one 60- or two 30-minute periods. Why this occurs is what exercise scientists call the "last bout" effect.

Your body responds in two ways to any type of exercise: you get both the extended "training response" and the immediate "biological response," both of which produce health benefits. A training response is a change in your body's structure or function from the exercise experience, which may be permanent or extended (for example, your muscles get bigger, your cardio-respiratory system uses oxygen more efficiently, etc.). The biological, or "last bout" response doesn't make any sort of permanent change in your body's structure or function, but it does have an immediate reaction to your exercise (for example, a drop in your blood pressure or release of endorphins into your bloodstream).

It's the last bout effect that people who regularly work out get "addicted" to all those warm, energised, positive feelings. Your mind and body are physically uplifted from getting your heart rate up, and good feelings spontaneously arise when endorphins are released. Still, we're not just getting the benefits of the classic "runner's high" here. Most of the time when you are regularly engaged in a health or fitness program, you are going to earn yourself effects that are a combination of both training *and* biological responses.

Here's a good example. If you are an older person with hypertension, and you work out on a stationary bike in the Healthy Heart zone for 15 minutes, you will probably see a significant drop in your systolic blood pressure for up to two hours after the exercise. That's a last bout effect. It's the result of the exercise experience, not of your accumulated training. What's great is that this biological response from the last exercise bout can be augmented by repeated regular bouts of exercise and can become permanent - a training response.

The bottom line? At relatively low exercise frequency and intensity, the body doesn't care about the kind of exercise or the duration or frequency of your workouts. What it does care about is your total exercise volume. Your body just really wants you to move around and spend a reasonable amount of energy in the health area of the wellness continuum. Your body doesn't care if you are raking leaves or shoveling snow or are on a cardiovascular machine at an athletic club. Your body doesn't discriminate against you if you are walking your dog or if you are a mail carrier. Your body only begs for one thing: that you move regularly and spend some energy. If you want to sip from the waters that Ponce de Leon did not taste, then dip your cup into the Healthy Heart zone.

A Z1 HEALTHY HEART WORKOUT

Starting a fitness program is a meaningful, literally *vital,* step; and you want to do so gently to allow your body to adjust to fitness. It's ypur choice whether you start out with ten minutes six days a week or twenty minutes three days a week for this workout. Your body will respond to each of them equivalently. Begin by putting on a pair of comfortable walking shoes and a casual outfit and choose a time of day that is going to be reliably convenient, when there is no competition for your attention.

Determine your specific numerical values for the Healthy Heart zone. If your Max HR is 200 then they will be from 100 to 120 bpm. (If you are using a heart rate monitor, you'll input these numbers as your zone's floor and ceiling.) Stretch for a couple of minutes and then start out walking slowly, smoothly picking up the pace to a brisk speed. It should take you about 60 seconds to break through the 100 bpm lower limit. About every minute or two you'll need to take your pulse rate or make a quick glance at your monitor (if it doesn't automatically beep at you when you go out of your zone) to ensure that you are within the zone. For at least the last two minutes of the workout make sure you are in the *upper* Healthy Heart zone, which would be 110-120 beats per minute if your Max HR were 200. At the end of the final two minutes, slow down for about sixty seconds to let your heart rate drop below the floor of your Healthy Heart zone. Sixty minutes a week. That's all. Hang out here for several weeks, and you'll get healthier.

The Z2 Temperate Zone

CHAPTER 8

As a life-long athlete, I've never had the sort of intimate relationship with the fat battle that some people have, but a woman named Lisa brought reality home to me with her experience.

"I was 135 pounds before the birth of my first daughter, but 210 pounds after the birth of my second. One day, though, my husband came home with a heart rate monitor. I'd heard about Z2 Heart Zone Training and decided to give it a try. I bounded into the Z2 zone and hung out there for one and one-half years, ate everything I wanted but limited my dietary fat intake to 30 grams a day, and the fat melted. I have maintained 135 pounds ever since." Lisa sustained a healthy weight loss amounting to about one pound per week.

WHAT IT DOES

The Z2 Temperate zone is so-called for a simple reason: It's a moderate and comfortable zone. As in the Healthy Heart zone, approximately 70%-85% of all of the calories that are burned in the Z2 zone come from fat. However, unlike the 4-6 calories or so per minute you can expect to burn in the Healthy Heart zone, in the Temperate zone an average person will burn about 6-10 calories per minute! So, in ten minutes of exercise, depending on your weight and other factors, you'll burn about 100 calories; and of these, approximately 85 calories will be from fat in your diet or your own body releasing its fat. (This blend will change to some degree based on your diet, current fitness, etc.)

As you continue to train into the higher zones, you will burn more calories, but you will also burn proportionately less fat as a percentage of your total calories.

The following summarises events and conditions within Z2:

Zone	Zone Name	% Max HR	Fuels Burned	Calories
Z2	Temperate	60–70%	10% Carbohydrates 85% Fat 5% Protein	±10 calories per minute

The chart below shows the percentage of foods burned:

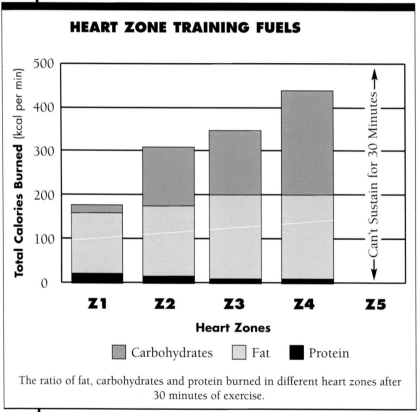

The ratio of fat, carbohydrates and protein burned in different heart zones after 30 minutes of exercise.

Adapted from Butterfield , Gail, et. al. Hershey Foods Corporation: Topics in Nutrition and Food Safety: Fuelling Activity, fall 1994, page 6

Is it better to burn more "absolute" calories during higher heart zone workouts, or to burn a higher percentage of your calories as fat calories in your three fat burning zones: Z1-Z3?

The answer is individual, depending totally on your fitness level and your goals. If you're already in shape, it's best to burn total calories; if you are on your way to getting fit, it's better to burn fat calories. If you're in great shape, you don't need to hang out in the fat burning zones, because you are fit not fat. If you are fat and not fit, this is the place for you.

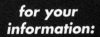

for your information:

Fat is our most abundant energy source. It is approximately fifty times more abundant in our bodies than carbohydrates.

By exercising in the temperate zone, you double your health rewards because you dispose of more body fat and, at the same time, gain muscle mass. Consequently you have more muscle available to burn fat and your resting metabolic rate increases. In other words, the more muscle mass you have, the more calories you'll burn just sitting still.

And, when you get into relatively good shape, you can hang out in zone 2 for a longer period of time - it can be a recovery zone or a long, slow endurance zone. If you use the Temperate zone for either purpose, then the blend of fuels your body burns becomes even more in your favor. With longer training sessions, more than 60 minutes in duration, your body begins to run out of the readily available carbohydrates in your system and relies even more on your body's stored fat. In the first few minutes of exercise, there is a tendency for the muscles to grab carbohydrates for fuel because they are readily available and don't have to be mobilised. This makes sense; when you first start up, you're body's looking for whatever it can get its hands on to stuff into the furnace. The longer the exercise duration, though, the more body fat that can be

When muscles demand energy to move, it takes time for your stored fat to break into smaller pieces so it can pass through the fat cell wall and into the bloodstream to be transported to your muscle cells.

broken down and shuttled out to the muscles via the blood-stream. That's what's so great about long, slow training - it increases your fat mobilisation.

Look at the chart below and you'll see how important fat is as a source of fuel during long work-outs.

EXERCISE TIME AND FUEL BURNED

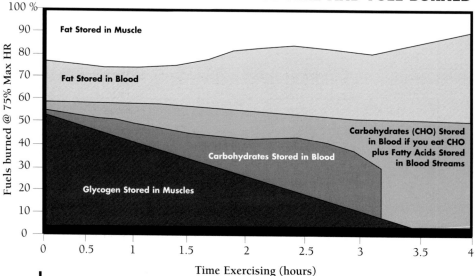

(Example: running a marathon, long triathlon, 100k bike ride or 50k ski)

HOW IT DOES IT

The floor for the Temperate zone is 60% Max HR, just above the Healthy Heart zone. The ceiling of the Z2 Temperate zone is 70% Max HR, just below the Aerobic zone. As you exercise in the Temperate zone you realise even more of the health benefits that accumulate from progressively moving from the Healthy Heart to the Temperate zone. Get beyond this zone, and you're achieving fitness more than health.

For someone whose maximum heart rate is 200 beats per minute (bpm), their Temperate zone is 120-140 bpm. This is a moderate level of activity, strenuous but challenging. It's that zone where you feel that you are working - you break a sweat early on but you can carry on a conversation the entire time and there isn't a feeling of discomfort.

Exercising in the Temperate zone allows your body to accomplish three things. Fat mobilisation is the first - getting the fat out of your cells. Fat is stored in fat cells as triglycerides, large molecules that can't pass through the cell wall into the bloodstream. When the muscles demand energy, as in exercise, the fat cells are stimulated by enzymes to divide the fat molecules into smaller pieces (fatty acids), which are then freely released into the bloodstream where they travel to the muscles. However, if your heart rate goes *above* the Temperate zone, more lactic acid is produced which begins to block the enzymes that allow the fat to be liberated from the cell. And, of course, trapped fat can't be burned.

The second accomplishment of the Temperate zone is getting the now-freed fatty acids not only out of the cells but into the bloodstream. This is where the lower training zones become even more important, because blood is still circulating in the fatty tissues at these lower heart rates. When you train in more intense heart rate zones, blood flow is restricted in fatty tissue. Therefore, even if the fat is released from the cells, it can't effectively enter the bloodstream.

Once in the bloodstream in sufficient concentrations, the free-floating fatty acids are drawn into the muscle fibres. Inside these fibres, the fatty acids are activated by more enzymes which prepare them to be broken down within the muscles' energy factories, the mitochondria.

It makes sense that the higher the concentration of free fatty acids, the more accessible they are for the muscles to utilise. However, mitochondria also depend on the presence of another player in the fat-burning process: oxygen. This is key: for fat to burn, oxygen must be present. If your heart rate goes too far above the Temperate zone, though, you end up training anaerobically, that is, "without oxygen." At these intensities, carbohydrates are burned, not fat.

These three steps in the process of fat loss - the release of fat from cells, the transportation of fat to the muscles, and the higher concentration of fatty acids combined with the availability of oxygen with which to burn the fat - happen far and away the most efficiently in the moderate intensities of the Temperate zone. In other words, hanging out in the Temperate zone allows you to open up your fat cells and let the fat come out.

GETTING BETTER ALL THE TIME

The benefits of exercising in the Temperate Z2 zone go on and on. Studies show that those who work out at low heart rates burn more fat, even when they are not in the midst of a training session, than do those who don't exercise. Training teaches the metabolic processes how to preferentially pick fat over sugar.

How does this happen? Remember when we talked about the training response in the last chapter? Working out in the Temperate zone causes these kinds of extended changes in your body's structure or function.

Specifically, the amount of stored fat you can burn is related to the rate at which you can supply fat to your muscles. When you increase the rate, you increase the percentage of fat burned. That's what training in the Temperate zone does - the more you train in the Temperate zone, the more efficient your body becomes at using fat for energy since, with exercise, there is an overall increase in the activity of the fat burning enzymes. this makes more fatty acids available leading to an increase in the availability of fat as the primary energy source.

There is another factor that determines the rate at which you can supply free fatty acids to be burned: the amount of blood flow to the muscle. When you engage in regular training, you increase the blood transport system's ability to deliver blood by increasing the number of capillaries surrounding the muscle fibres, so more blood flows to your muscles. Training in the Temperate zone allows you to increase the amount of free fatty acids released out of your cells and into your bloodstream as well as to increase the amount of blood flow to your muscles.

Also, by training in the Temperate zone, you substantially increase the number of mitochondria in each muscle fibre. Since fat combustion takes place in the mitochondria, the more you have of these small energy factories, the more fat calories you can burn. Next, the size of the mitochondria increase with exercise. With bigger energy factories – mitochondria – you can combust even more fat calories. Research has shown that mitochondria get about 35% bigger with training, while there can be as much as a 15% increase in the quantity of mitochondria.

The mitochondrial enzymes' activity increases, too. Increasing this activity increases the mitochondria's efficiency and, thus, the muscles' aerobic capacity (your ability to utilise oxygen). With an increase in the number, the size, *and* the activity of the mitochondria, the Fat Burner is well-equipped to release, transport, and burn more and more fat as a source of energy.

As you hang out in the different zones, another one of your body's training responses is to increase the amount of your muscle tissue or lean body mass. You want this. The more muscle mass you have, the more calories you burn at rest and your resting metabolic rate, the amount of calories you burn by just being alive, increases.

None of these changes happen overnight, so don't expect to start a Heart Zone Training program and see improvements on your second day. When you add a weight loss component to your training there usually isn't immediate weight loss. This is normal. We often think we can "beat the system." We can't.

for your information:

Triglycerides are the form in which fat occurs both in foods and in the body's fat cells.

Heart Zone Training works within the system, optimizing the way the body works.

At some point as you increase the intensity of your exercise, as your heart rate approaches your maximum, your muscles shift to using a higher percentage of carbohydrates than fats. This intensity level is called the "cross-over point." That is, as your heart rate increases, the muscles cross over from using mostly fat as their energy source to pre-dominantly carbohydrates. One of the definitions of fitness is to change this crossover point to a higher heart rate or a higher training load. That is, as you get fitter you burn more total fat calories at lower heart rate numbers than when you are less fit.

In the old school, exercise consultants preached the philosophy of "LSD" workouts. Now, before you start thinking that all those runners out there in the '70s were so stoned out of their minds that it was a miracle they weren't tripping over their own feet, let me clarify. To us, "LSD" stood for "Long, Slow Distances." We did twenty a day'ers - twenty *miles* a day of running - as frequent workouts. We were convinced that the longer we ran, the more fat we would burn (which is, in fact, true) and that this was one of the tracks of the road to true runners' high. We ran and ran and ran for years and years and years. But, as students of both our experience and of ongoing academic research, we began to cut back, Heart Zone Train, run fewer miles, *and* set more personal bests. We learned the Heart Zone Training lesson, that the quality could be more important than the quantity of our exercise.

Today we've entered the era of SSDs - short, slow distances. That's really what the Temperate zone is, at least in the beginning. The results are huge on the health continuum as well as in the mind.

So, how do you put the Z2 into practice? Do what a friend of mine named Sharon does four times a week - twenty-a-day'ers. She loves a variety of cross-training, so in the summer she swims one day, circuit trains in gym for one, bikes another, and walk-runs a fourth – each for twenty minutes, and each in the Temperate zone. In the winter, one day a week she circuit trains for 20 minutes, the next she sport snowshoes for 20 minutes, the third she cross-country skis, and on the fourth she uses a stair-stepper or treadmill machine. Twenty minutes, four times a week is enough to melt the fat away, so long as it's twenty minutes in the Temperate zone.

Each time, she burns fat calories as her primary fuel source, even though she doesn't burn as many total calories as if she were in the Aerobic zone. And she enjoys the workout because it's fun and not painful. Because of the variety, she keeps her motivation and interest high. Each time she knows that she is investing in her health – the most important thing she has in her life.

Remember, though, training in the Temperate zone is only half of the fat-loss game plan. If you eat a high fat diet, then your fat cells are competing with what you just ate as the source of fat for energy. Muscle fibres prefer dietary fat over stored body fat, after all.

Z2 Temperate Zone 60% - 70% Maximum Heart Rate Chart

Max HR	150	155	160	165	170	175	180	185	190	195	200	205	210 bpm
60%	90	93	96	99	102	105	108	111	114	117	120	123	125
70%	105	109	112	116	119	123	126	130	133	137	140	143	146

without sophisticated equipment found only in an exercise physiology or research laboratory.

SELF-TESTING YOUR ANAEROBIC THRESHOLD

Outside a laboratory setting, there are a few methods which you can use to estimate your anaerobic threshold number. The qualification you need to remember about AT HR, though, is that it's a moving target, which means as you get fitter, it gets higher. As you train, your body will be able to utilise more oxygen and better metabolise fuels so you can work at higher heart rates more comfortably. It's an indication that your AT HR is moving towards your Max HR when you feel the same pace is getting easier. This is all great stuff, but it does mean that if you are going to have an anaerobic threshold number you can use for more than a couple of weeks, you're going to have to keep testing yourself at regular intervals.

• Sustainable Pace Heart Rate AT HR Test.

From the thousands of people tested on his treadmills, Dave Martin, Ph.D. (author of *Training Distance Runners*) has deduced that your 5 K racing pace (or a race of about 20 minutes in duration in any sport) is from 3-5 beats above your AT HR if you are exerting yourself totally. Using his test, to determine your AT HR value, you need to run, bike, ski, five kilometres and, after the first five minutes, start looking at your heart rate monitor. During the early minutes of a race, your heart rate is influenced by pre-race syndrome and doesn't immediately respond to the rapid increase in workload. Towards the end of the race, you tend to get even more competitive and drive your heart rate towards maximum. Take this middle-of-the-race average heart rate and subtract 5 beats to determine your AT HR. You can even calculate the percentage of your Max HR if you have completed that test.

Average 5K Race Heart Rate: _____ bpm
Minus five beats: **-5** bpm
Approximate Anaerobic Threshold HR Number: _____ bpm

• **Perceived Exertion AT HR Test.** This method uses your "feeling" of intensity level - the "rating of perceived exertion" - combined with your fitness level. Select a treadmill or a bike and proceed with the warm-up phase. After an adequate warm-up, begin a ladder of one-minute intensity increases of 50 Watts on the bike or 1/2 mph or 1% grade on the treadmill. Use this one-step increase per minute until you feel that the exercise load is "hard" or "difficult." It should not be too difficult to continue, but hard enough that you say "I only feel I can do this for another 10–20 minutes at this level." The entire test should take no more than 10–15 minutes and you will have a fairly accurate AT HR at the point when you feel that the workload is "very hard." If you are at a highly competitive level, use the feeling that the workload is "very, very hard."

When you self-test, look first at your fitness category and then the subjective feeling that fits this category. For example, if you classify yourself as "fit" then your AT HR is at about or around the number 8 and between "very hard" and "very, very hard." To use these values as a way of calculating your Max HR, take your AT HR and add 15-30 bpm to it for Max HR.

Rating of Perceived Exertion

Perceived Exertion (RPE)	Feeling	Sedentary	Individual Fit	SuperFit
1	Rest			
2	Very weak			
3	Moderate			
4	Somewhat hard			
5	Hard	•		
6		•		
7	Very Hard		•	
8			•	
9				•
10	Very, Very Hard			•

Wondering which marvellous activity to turn to? Choose any of them, and do as many of the indoor and outdoor sports as your fun-loving inner child desires; just remember it's the zones (and the amount of time you spend in them) that matter.

THE TRANSITION ZONE

The Aerobic zone has very specific parameters. The aerobic zone floor is 70% of your maximum heart rate (Max HR) and it is at this point that you begin to realise substantial cardiovascular benefits. If your true Max HR were tested at 200 bpm, then the aerobic floor heart rate for your purposes would be 140 bpm.

Its neighbouring zone to the lower side is the Temperate zone. Once you cross over from the Temperate to the Aerobic zone, it doesn't mean that you stop burning fat as a source of calories. It just means that the percentage of types of fuels burned changes. No longer are you burning the vast majority of your calories from fats; instead you're shifting into the zones that use more carbohydrates as their fuel source.

The ceiling for the Aerobic zone is 80% of your Max HR. This is actually quite strenuous for the novice exerciser. For someone who has been training for a few weeks or months, this might be considered "somewhat hard" or "hard" if you were to give the feeling a verbal description. Above the ceiling of the Aerobic zone is the Threshold zone. When you cross this line you've entered the world of performance training. If your true Max HR were tested at 200 bpm, then your aerobic ceiling heart rate would be 160 bpm. This Aerobic heart rate zone is also known as the "talk test zone" because it is within this zone that you can speak without a shortness of breath or loss of words; if you start to exercise above it, however, a friendly chat soon becomes the last thing on your mind.

The Aerobic zone is the fitness area at the heart of the wellness continuum. It is the transition zone between the two health zones and the two performance zones. It's also the first of the zones where performance training effects begin. In the Aerobic zone you begin to realise the changes that lead to athletic conditioning versus basic health and fitness. That is, this is the zone where tremendous (but somewhat technical) physiological changes occur. As indicated below, the cardiopulmonary changes from rest to the aerobic level are enormous.

	Active Rest (sitting quietly)	Aerobic Zone (70-80% Max HR)
Heart Rate:	30-80 bpm	120-180 bpm
Oxygen Utilisation	3.5 ml/kg/min	50 ml/kg/min
Respiratory Rate:	12 breaths/min	35-45 breaths/min
Expired Airflow	5 L/min	180 L/min
Cardiac Output	5 L/min	40 L/min
Working Muscles Blood Flow	1.2 L/min	12 L/min
Blood Flow to Kidneys	1.1 L/min	6 L/min
Heat Production	100 kcal/hr	1,000 kcal/hr

The changes are incredible - it's a comfort zone. (Don't forget - it's also comfortable.) The Aerobic zone is where you break sweat, raising your core temperature to just above the sweat point, but not much beyond. You feel like you have had a workout when you train here, but you don't feel any of the burn or the pain. If you do, you have pushed yourself through the Aerobic ceiling and into the anaerobic Threshold zone, which isn't the place to be if your goal is to achieve fitness. It feels great to take a shower after an Aerobic zone workout because you can feel that you have released both emotionally and physically some of your stored-up toxins. The Aerobic zone is a place where you get a lot of rewards and feel good about both your mental and your physical muscles. Quite simply, when you are

The following summarises events and conditions within Z3:

Zone	Zone Name	% Max HR	Fuels Burned	Calories
Z3	Aerobic	70–80%	60% Carbohydrates 35% Fat 5% Protein	±6 calories per minute

Comment. What you are trying to accomplish with this workout is to push your AT HR up toward to your Max HR and then step back on the throttle just enough to breathe more comfortably before you push up to your AT again.

This isn't an easy workout. Your first time you might just try one main set. By the end of your training program you might want to try three sets. It is definitely a challenge and you will feel it the following day. The next morning make sure you take your resting HR before you get out of bed to make sure you have not pushed yourself too hard the day before. The next day's workout needs to be a recovery or a Temperate Zone day.

The Z5 Redline Zone

If you've made it to the Redline zone, with heart rates from 90% to 100% of your Max HR, you have arrived at the top of the heap. Maybe we should say, if you've made it to the Z5 Redline zone *on purpose*. Like the Threshold zone, this is another one of those places that most people end up visiting only unwittingly: chasing their escaped dog or cat down the street, or running to catch their train, plane, or boat. You remember. This is the place where your heart feels like it's going to burst and your legs soon feel like lead. While no one would ever want to live there, the vast majority of us wouldn't even call the Redline zone a nice place to visit.

If you've arrived at the Redline zone on purpose, you're one of a proud, perhaps crazy, minority. It's a place I love. I love to eat lactates. I love to go hard. I love to see how long, how fast, how high I can go. It's that place where we suffer excruciatingly from metabolic processes. It's the place for masochistic athletes. Quite frankly, it's wonderful - for me.

You simply can't hang out for long periods of time in the Redline zone without dropping out of it for a breather. Your heart rate cannot hang out at or near maximum, because of its exceedingly high demand for fuels. Every second you are in the Redline zone, your body's oxygen and glycogen needs exceed your ability to deliver them. The heart muscle is a "work now, pay now" muscle, and it will not go into oxygen debt. Because skeletal muscles operate under the principle of "work now and pay later," they have the ability to keep on going, past the balance point, and drive themselves into oxygen and glycogen debt. And what is the key to the skeletal muscles' deferment of metabolic

CARDIO IMPROVEMENTS

If you were shocked at the amount of unfamiliar exercise terminology before, you'd better steel yourself, because it gets worse before it gets better. Once you enter the fitness and performance zones, you start hearing people toss around long and impressive words, like "cardiovascular" or "cardiopulmonary," or short and weird ones, like "VO$_2$ max" (but more on that later).

Taking the roots of the first word, "cardio" for heart and "vascular," referring to your blood vessels, this is the zone that works the heart and its blood-transport system. The Aerobic zone gives us cardiopulmonary - referring to both the heart and the lungs - benefits, too. In reality, all three parts - heart and lung and vessels - are simultaneously worked by the wonderful Aerobic zone.

How many actually know what "aerobic" means? Well, literally, "aerobic" means "with air." In fitness terms it means that you are exercising at an intensity level such that the lungs can infuse sufficient oxygen into the blood, while the heart can pump sufficient quantities of the oxygen-laden blood to all of the muscles - including the heart muscle.

Some of the cardiovascular improvements that your body undergoes as a result of Aerobic zone exercise are:
An increase in the number and size of blood vessels, resulting in
- increased blood delivery to your muscles,
- increased oxygen delivery to the muscles for fuel,
- increased oxygen delivery to the fat cells to free them into the blood,
- increased blood to carry the fat from fat cells to the muscles,
- increased number of mitochondria within muscle cells that convert fuels for muscle combustion,
- increased size of each individual mitochondria,
- increased number of capillaries in the working muscles,
- increased size of existing capillaries,
- increased size of coronary arteries,
- reduction in blood pressure.

An increase in both the size and strength of the heart, resulting in increased stroke volume (the amount of blood pumped with each heartbeat),
- increased cardiac output (stroke volume times heart rate),
- decreased heart rate for the same intensity level training load.
- an increase in red blood cell volume, plasma volume, and total blood volume.

Some of the cardiopulmonary or respiratory changes that result from training in the Aerobic zone are:
- Increased vital capacity (the amount of air that can be breathed out after a maximal intake of breath).
- Decreased respiratory rate (the number of breaths you take in response to a given level of training load).
- Increased maximal pulmonary ventilation (the volume of oxygen per minute you can breathe).
- Increased pulmonary diffusion (the amount of oxygen exchanged by the lungs).
- Increased difference in arterial-venous oxygen (more oxygen is extracted at the tissue level).

VO$_2$ MAX

Another value of the Aerobic zone is that if you train in Z3 your VO$_2$ max will improve. This rather cryptic benefit may not mean much to you if you are unfamiliar with fitness jargon, so let me explain. The more oxygen that you absorb and feed to your muscles, the better you will be able to exercise. With increased oxygen utilisation at a given intensity level, your heart rate at that training load will be lower. Why? Your heart rate increases to provide more oxygenated blood to your muscles, but if you've trained your body to the point where it's already circulating more oxygen, your heart isn't going to need to work harder. *That* is a key definition of aerobic fitness improvement, and it is one of the primary benefits of the Aerobic zone.

Exercise scientists have devised a way of measuring the quantity of oxygen that your muscles burn and the quantity of carbon dioxide that they release as one of the byproducts of

Our skeletal muscles love glucose or, as we like to think of it, "muscle sugar." Glucose, when it is burned at high-intensity heart rates, is chemically transformed into lactates which, as we know, are acids. It's the build-up of these acids which leads to acidosis, that tell-tale feeling of overall fatigue, heavily wooden limbs, hard breathing, and burning muscle pain.

REDLINING AND OVERTRAINING

If you want to get fast, you have to train fast. It's a standard rule that SSD (short slow distance) and LSD (long slow distance) workouts aren't valuable as anything but recovery workouts for the individual training for high performance. However, the Redline zone is so hot that an overdose or miscalculation in training here can result in long-term damage and the need for long-term recovery.

There are some serious consequences of hanging out too long in this zone. First, with the high levels of acidosis from the presence of lactic acid, muscle cell enzymes are affected. That is, the enzymes that are responsible for aerobic metabolism are sabotaged, and one's aerobic endurance capacity is hurt. Repeated days of high intensity redlining results in damage to these enzymes, and you simply can't train aerobically without problems.

What really happens is that the lactic acid damages the muscle cell wall. Like any wall, the damaged muscle cell wall breaks down, and the cell material leaks out into the blood. That's when you see increases in certain blood panel concentrations like urea and CPK. It means that the walls are leaking.

for your information:

The purest of the forms of glycogen is ATP, or adenosine triphosphate. When you are in the Redline Zone and sprinting a 100-yard dash, you are burning principally ATP. Here's the catch - we only have enough ATP available in storage for about 10 seconds, before it's exhausted, Clearly ATP is not a fuel to be dependent on - it burns off as fast as it takes a match to burn out.

If you don't heed the warning signs and do some training in the lower zones - or simply rest - your ability to train will continue to diminish substantially, because a cell wall takes a long time to recover.

Among the common negative outcomes of too much time in the Redline zone:

• **Interference with coordination capacity.** In sports like soccer, skiing, martial arts, basketball, and ice skating, where both endurance and coordination are requirements, there is little to no improvement in technical skills when the individual is exposed to the upper Redline zone and near exhaustion. High lactic acid contents in the blood interfere with coordination, lessening the benefits of training, not increasing them.

• **Increased red blood cell destruction rate.** Red blood cells are responsible for carrying oxygen, and their health and numerical stability in the bloodstream is obviously of vital importance to anyone, let alone the endurance athlete. Yet, when training in the Redline zone, acidosis causes the membranes of red blood cells to become unstable, which makes them more fragile. This fragility is augmented by the number of red blood cells that are destroyed because of mechanical trauma and the increased speed of the blood flow into small capillary vessels.

• **Increased risk of injuries.** High acidosis within the muscle tissues result in weakening of the muscles to such an extent that severe muscle injuries occur more readily.

• **Diminished ATP energy renewal.** Again because of the high concentration of lactic acid, ATP, the energy source for short bursts, does not reformulate as quickly. This delay in reformation severely limits one's ability to perform short sprints of exercise during training sessions.

• **Damage to aerobic capacity.** The lactic acidosis also causes damage to endurance capacity because it interferes number of beats per minute for the music) and watch your heart rate change. Throughout the entire time you should be above your Aerobic zone floor yet never break through the Aerobic ceiling.

At the second session, keep the music intensity the same but add one more riser, making your step 8". Now, determine the heart rate cost of adding that 4 inches of step height. For most, this equates to a 5–10 beat increase in average heart rate (if you have a heart rate monitor, measure the difference in the average as well as the high and low heart rate values). If it results in an increase of more than an average of 15-25 beats per minute, this is a clear indication that your current fitness level could use some improving. It also means that you should take the second riser off and go back to a lower step level in order to stay in your Aerobic zone.

On the third exercise session if you haven't already gone through the Aerobic ceiling, add the final riser, which should make your step 12", while keeping the choreography and the music identical. The only change will be in your step height. Again, measure your change in heart rate and adjust your step height accordingly for next time. After three sessions, you should have a pretty good idea of which step height gave you the best Aerobic zone workout, but keep in mind that as your fitness increases, you'll need to start adding steps again, and retesting yourself.

Variations of this workout include mixing the choreography as well as the music cadence. Play with these variables and teach yourself how to change your zones (perhaps working through both your Z2 *and* Z3 zones in one workout) by varying the elements of your training load - music beat, resistance as step height, and chore-ography - to enjoy multiple training effects.

The Z4 Threshold Zone

Welcome to the Threshold zone! Even if you don't choose to train in the Z4 Threshold zone, it's a place you're no doubt familiar with, though maybe you are unfamiliar with its name. Here's a hint: this is also known as the "shortness of breath" zone. Sound familiar? It's the zone where you feel the burn in your legs as you quickly climb a set of stairs; where, when you reach the top, lean over, put your hands on your thighs and try to catch your breath, your mind slowly reminds you, "You're really out of shape."

The Threshold zone is so-called because, for most *fit* people, within this zone of 80-90% Max HR is your anaerobic threshold. This is where you pass from aerobic metabolism, which means with oxygen, to anaerobic metabolism, meaning without oxygen. Above the anaerobic threshold, oxygen debt starts to rapidly accumulate and lactates are spewing out. It can be a very uncomfortable place. But here's the startling part about the anaerobic threshold. In the *unfit* individual, it is common to see anaerobic thresholds at around 60% of their Max HR. And, in the extremely fit, it is common to see anaerobic thresholds above 90% of their Max HR. The chart below gives you a view of the parts of Z4.

This is very important: if you are unfit and your anaerobic threshold heart rate point is within your fat burning zones, you *can't* train in the Threshold zone. It's simply too high a heart rate intensity. You need to stay below your anaerobic threshold for *all* of your exercise; hence, the Healthy Heart zone is perfect. This is the primary reason why exercise fails the healthy unfit: we're asking them to train far above their anaerobic thresholds.

attempting to answer the fatigue question. In my athletic years, I have trained and raced in some of the longest and hardest races in the world in a continuing attempt to understand what makes us exhausted and what we can do about it.

The personal reason I want to find the source of fatigue is to combat it - to override it so we can go further and faster. It's a truism that love-hate relationships are the most dangerous. You thirst for the love and suffer from the hate, and together the ambivalence can drive you crazy. For me (and others!) the Redline zone is exactly that same relationship. You thirst for the benefits (enhanced performance) and suffer from the experience (pain), and together they can drive you to stardom or failure.

Still, because it is difficult, if not downright dangerous, to hang out for any length of time in the Redline zone, it is time that needs to be carefully planned. We stay there for a short time, then recover and hop back into it. Then it's out to rest again. This is called interval training, and there are actually two types of intervals: the exercise interval and the rest interval. The exercise or training interval is the amount of time that we spend at a certain heart rate or workload. The rest interval is the time that we spend recovering from the exercise interval.

For example, let's say you want to do lower Redline zone intervals (90–95% Max HR). You could do short, or "sprint" intervals (rather than middle or long intervals) of one minute at that heart rate, with a one-minute active recovery interval. That's called a 1:1 ratio of effort to rest, because you are spending equal amounts of time (a minute each, in this case) exercising and resting.

Z5 Redline Zone 90% - 100% Maximum Heart Rate Chart

Max HR	150	155	160	165	170	175	180	185	190	195	200	205	210 bpm
90%	135	140	144	149	153	158	162	167	171	176	180	184	189
100%	150	155	160	165	170	175	180	185	190	195	200	205	210

If your Max HR were 200 bpm, then to do this lower Redline workout you would exercise in a narrow zone of 180-190 bpm for one minute. Then you'd slow considerably and rest, still moving (this is an *active* rest), letting your heart rate drop for one minute. Each group of one minute in Z5 and one minute out of Redline is the "interval set." You may choose to do 6-10 of these sets for your workout.

This Redline workout can be done on a track, on a bike, nordic skiing, running, or swimming.

In your monitor, set the upper zone to 95% of your true Max HR. In the case of someone whose Max HR is 200, they would set the monitor to 190 beats per minute. Next set the monitor's alarm to sound at every one minute. Use an active recovery of 30-60 seconds by walking, gliding or slow pedalling before you begin the next interval. Break the workout into two sets of five different 1:1 interval repeats, with a 3-5 minute rest between each set.

The reason you want active recovery between the exercise interval is to sustain high levels of lactates in your blood. That's one of the main purposes of the workout - lactate tolerance training. You are trying to build up your lactate concentrations during the session. When there is too much recovery, your lactates drop. If you can't finish 5 repeats the first couple of tries, that's fine. Start with 2-4 and build your way up.

There is a slight delay between your real heart rate and the monitor reading. That's because your heart rate is higher than the monitor because it is updating the data each 5 seconds, so it is always delayed - on both the active and the recovery times. This lagging of your monitor behind your true heart rate is one of the drawbacks to the technology as it exists today. In the near future there will be real-time heart rate monitors. But for now be satisfied that the data is so close (far better than you could derive from taking your pulse) and remember that we are only listening for the alarm as we accelerate our heart rate into the Redline zone.

For runners who like track workouts, two of my favourites are called ladders and "dropping 1 second per quarter." Both add new dimensions to an already overtaxing experience. With ladders, change the heart rate ceiling by 2 beats (or 1%) per lap.

number. For example, if I can run a 10K at my maximum sustainable heart rate of 175 bpm, for me that is 85% of my maximum heart rate.

The most obvious question is what kind of training is necessary to improve the anaerobic threshold heart rate and maximum sustainable heart rate? For the answer, you would need to jump forward to Chapter 12 ("High Performance with Heart Zone Training"). For here, the brief answer is called the "At/About/ Around" Principle. That is, a large percentage of your "time in zone" needs to be at/about/around your anaerobic threshold heart rate - up to 25%-50% of your training time if you are training to race competitively in the final training period.

Keep in mind, too, that your anaerobic threshold heart rate (AT HR) number is specific to the activity in which you are engaged. If your AT HR is 185 bpm running, it might well be 178 bpm cycling. It is postulated that these differences are related to the muscle mass used during the specific activities, as well as whether the activity is weight-bearing or not. AT HR is not only sport-specific, it is conditioned sport-specific. If you are currently fit running and unfit swimming, you can have a high AT HR for running and a low AT HR for swimming.

Triathletes are great examples of Threshold zone aficionados. We love to hammer as much as possible and to constantly test ourselves in all three sports: swimming, cycling, and running. When I first began doing triathlons in the early '80s, there was little to nothing written on cross-training or multi-sport programs. So, using the laboratory of the self and what little available research I could find, I decided to devise a self-test to determine my anaerobic threshold. Each week I took this self test in one of the three disciplines, and, as the weeks went by, I watched my scores improve.

THE ANAEROBIC AND LACTATE THRESHOLDS

The history of the term "anaerobic threshold" dates back to 1923, when two exercise scientists, Doctors Hill and Lupton, first noticed that when skeletal muscles are subjected to increasing training loads their metabolic demands exceeded what the body could provide to them. It wasn't until 1964, when the testing equipment became available to measure oxygen and carbon dioxide consumption and blood lactate changes, that the anaerobic threshold first became accurately determinable. Karl Wasserman used the term "anaerobic threshold" to define a particular training load where blood lactates first begin to rise above their resting levels. Since then, the meaning has evolved to refer to that region of change where lactates increase dramatically rather than moderately.

Of course, the controversy over the "true" definition of anaerobic threshold continues today. In brief, it appears that there are two thresholds, not one, and both are related to a rise in lactic acid serum concentrations. One is a small rise in blood lactates and breathing changes from mild work, commonly measured at about 2.0 mm/L. This is now commonly thought to be an a<u>er</u>obic threshold. The names researchers use for it include "the onset of plasma lactate accumulation," "the first threshold," "the aerobic threshold," and so on. The bottom line is that it closely corresponds with the Aerobic zone heart rate floor.

The other threshold, that is observed with more intense exercise, consists of a rapid accumulation of blood lactates and more substantial breathing changes. This is thought to be the anaerobic threshold and is commonly measured at about 4.0 mm/L. This second threshold has just as many different labels as the first, including "lactate turn point," "OBLA" (onset of blood lactate accumulation), "the individual anaerobic threshold," "the second threshold," "the respiratory compensation for metabolic acidosis threshold," "the lactate/ventilatory threshold," etc. For our purposes, we won't be differentiating among the names - we'll just use the term "anaerobic threshold."

It is this second, anaerobic threshold that is of critical importance to those who train for performance. The reason is that it's a trainable heart rate number, providing a readily measurable test of fitness improvement. It also might be a more accurate way to set heart zones, but is not generally used for this because it isn't possible to accurately measure the anaerobic threshold without sophisticated equipment found only in an exercise physiology or research laboratory.

SELF-TESTING YOUR ANAEROBIC THRESHOLD

Outside a laboratory setting, there are a few methods which you can use to estimate your anaerobic threshold number. The qualification you need to remember about AT HR, though, is that it's a moving target, which means as you get fitter, it gets higher. As you train, your body will be able to utilise more oxygen and better metabolise fuels so you can work at higher heart rates more comfortably. It's an indication that your AT HR is moving towards your Max HR when you feel the same pace is getting easier. This is all great stuff, but it does mean that if you are going to have an anaerobic threshold number you can use for more than a couple of weeks, you're going to have to keep testing yourself at regular intervals.

• Sustainable Pace Heart Rate AT HR Test.

From the thousands of people tested on his treadmills, Dave Martin, Ph.D. (author of *Training Distance Runners*) has deduced that your 5 K racing pace (or a race of about 20 minutes in duration in any sport) is from 3-5 beats above your AT HR if you are exerting yourself totally. Using his test, to determine your AT HR value, you need to run, bike, ski, five kilometres and, after the first five minutes, start looking at your heart rate monitor. During the early minutes of a race, your heart rate is influenced by pre-race syndrome and doesn't immediately respond to the rapid increase in workload. Towards the end of the race, you tend to get even more competitive and drive your heart rate towards maximum. Take this middle-of-the-race average heart rate and subtract 5 beats to determine your AT HR. You can even calculate the percentage of your Max HR if you have completed that test.

Average 5K Race Heart Rate:	_____ bpm
Minus five beats:	**-5** bpm
Approximate Anaerobic Threshold HR Number:	_____ bpm

• **Perceived Exertion AT HR Test.** This method uses your "feeling" of intensity level - the "rating of perceived exertion" - combined with your fitness level. Select a treadmill or a bike and proceed with the warm-up phase. After an adequate warm-up, begin a ladder of one-minute intensity increases of 50 Watts on the bike or 1/2 mph or 1% grade on the treadmill. Use this one-step increase per minute until you feel that the exercise load is "hard" or "difficult." It should not be too difficult to continue, but hard enough that you say "I only feel I can do this for another 10–20 minutes at this level." The entire test should take no more than 10–15 minutes and you will have a fairly accurate AT HR at the point when you feel that the workload is "very hard." If you are at a highly competitive level, use the feeling that the workload is "very, very hard.

When you self-test, look first at your fitness category and then the subjective feeling that fits this category. For example, if you classify yourself as "fit" then your AT HR is at about or around the number 8 and between "very hard" and "very, very hard." To use these values as a way of calculating your Max HR, take your AT HR and add 15-30 bpm to it for Max HR.

Rating of Perceived Exertion

Perceived Exertion (RPE)	Feeling	Sedentary	Individual Fit	SuperFit
1	Rest			
2	Very weak			
3	Moderate			
4	Somewhat hard			
5	Hard	•		
6		•		
7	Very Hard		•	
8			•	
9				•
10	Very, Very Hard			•

Here are some words to help explain the language used to equate a numerical value to RPE:

RPE	Feeling	Words
4	Somewhat hard	You could probably keep this up for a very long time.
5	Hard	Respiration deeper, challenging yet still comfortable, you can continue.
7	Very Hard	Tough but breathing is still rhythmic
10	Very, Very Hard	You are breathing fast and ready to stop, you can't talk and it's a struggle to maintain the pace.

Workout #6:
ANAEROBIC THRESHOLD WORKOUT: AT-ABOUT-AROUND

Introduction. It is difficult to sustain your anaerobic threshold heart rate for longer than about 20-60 minutes in any single activity. (Remember AT HR is sports specific). The closer you can race at or above your AT HR the higher your achievable maximum sustainable HR (MS HR). And, the higher your MS HR is, the faster you can race.

Workout Plan. This workout can apply to almost any activity but it is not for the beginner. It is based on the principle that the AT HR number is an individual HR buried in the centre of a very,

very narrow HR window or zone. For this workout, the zone is five beats, with a top number or ceiling of your AT HR and the bottom or floor of the workout zone five beats lower.

The workout is two by 20 minutes. After warming up take yourself up to your AT HR and hold "at-about-around" that number for two minutes, then drop five beats to your floor and hold for two minutes. Cross back and forth every two minutes between this narrow window for 20 continuous minutes. Do an active recovery for five minutes then repeat the main set before a warm-down.

Workout Example. This is what the workout would look like for someone who has an AT HR of 185 beats per minute (bpm). If you don't know your AT HR, use your average HR during the middle of a 5K race.

Warm-up: 5 minutes up to 140 bpm.

Main Set:

2 minutes at 185 bpm

2 minutes at 180 bpm

2 minutes at 185 bpm

2 minutes at 180 bpm

2 minutes at 185 bpm

2 minutes at 180 bpm

2 minutes at 185 bpm

2 minutes at 180 bpm

2 minutes at 185 bpm

2 minutes at 180 bpm

Active Rest: 5 minutes at 145 bpm

Repeat Main Set

Warm-down: 5 minutes at 145 bpm

Comment. What you are trying to accomplish with this workout is to push your AT HR up toward to your Max HR and then step back on the throttle just enough to breathe more comfortably before you push up to your AT again.

This isn't an easy workout. Your first time you might just try one main set. By the end of your training program you might want to try three sets. It is definitely a challenge and you will feel it the following day. The next morning make sure you take your resting HR before you get out of bed to make sure you have not pushed yourself too hard the day before. The next day's workout needs to be a recovery or a Temperate Zone day.

The Z5 Redline Zone

If you've made it to the Redline zone, with heart rates from 90% to 100% of your Max HR, you have arrived at the top of the heap. Maybe we should say, if you've made it to the Z5 Redline zone *on purpose*. Like the Threshold zone, this is another one of those places that most people end up visiting only unwittingly: chasing their escaped dog or cat down the street, or running to catch their train, plane, or boat. You remember. This is the place where your heart feels like it's going to burst and your legs soon feel like lead. While no one would ever want to live there, the vast majority of us wouldn't even call the Redline zone a nice place to visit.

If you've arrived at the Redline zone on purpose, you're one of a proud, perhaps crazy, minority. It's a place I love. I love to eat lactates. I love to go hard. I love to see how long, how fast, how high I can go. It's that place where we suffer excruciatingly from metabolic processes. It's the place for masochistic athletes. Quite frankly, it's wonderful - for me.

You simply can't hang out for long periods of time in the Redline zone without dropping out of it for a breather. Your heart rate cannot hang out at or near maximum, because of its exceedingly high demand for fuels. Every second you are in the Redline zone, your body's oxygen and glycogen needs exceed your ability to deliver them. The heart muscle is a "work now, pay now" muscle, and it will not go into oxygen debt. Because skeletal muscles operate under the principle of "work now and pay later," they have the ability to keep on going, past the balance point, and drive themselves into oxygen and glycogen debt. And what is the key to the skeletal muscles' deferment of metabolic payment, their ability to keep on contracting without fuel in sight? The (extremely high) production of lactates.

Lactic acid junkies like me love hanging out in the Redline zone because we get faster while training at the same heart rate or intensity. Since the Z5 zone is the outermost zone in the heart zone chart, sitting just above Z4, this means that all of your time spent in the Redline zone is at a heart rate that is higher than your anaerobic threshold heart rate (if your AT HR is less than 90% of your Max HR). After all, the best way to improve your anaerobic threshold is to train at-about-around your anaerobic threshold heart rate. This zone is also affectionately known as the "lactate tolerance zone" because this is the zone that conditions the body to buffer or withstand the high acidosis as well as to shuttle away the lactic acid to be resynthesized.

It's in the Redline zone that you squarely, up front and with no way around, it meet your maximum heart rate. When you see your maximum heart rate, know that exhaustion - complete and total exhaustion - is no more than a minute away. Very soon, you will quite simply peter out. Z5 is a dangerous place, because if you don't come visit often enough you can't reach your peak, but if you overstay your visit your body won't invite you to return.

The Redline zone is feared by many and misunderstood by more. One of the most frequently asked questions about Heart Zone Training applies here: are the benefits cumulative?

Why do we use our Max HR numbers as the anchor point for zones rather than anaerobic or lactate threshold?

♥ MAX/HR

Answer: We do this because maximum heart rate is a fixed number so we can fix the five zones. Anaerobic threshold heart rate changes with conditioning, so as you get fitter, it goes higher. Because AT HR number moves with conditioning, all of your zones also change with conditioning. With each beat of change in anaerobic heart rate, there is a change in all of the floors and ceilings of all of the zones. The use of maximum HR is, therefore, more practical and less confusing.

In other words, if you hang out in Z5, are you going to get all of the benefits from the Healthy Heart, Temperate, Aerobic and Threshold zone The answer is no. In each zone, a different process occurs that is specific to that process; if you want to receive that benefit, then you have to pay your dues in that zone.

The following summarises events and conditions within Z5:

Zone	Zone Name	% Max HR	Fuels Burned	Calories
Z5	Redline	90–100%	90% Carbohydrates 5% Fat 5% Protein	±20 calories per minute

REDLINE FUELS

For those wanting to burn off a high percentage of fat calories, the Redline is one of those zones that won't help you in the slightest. In the Redline zone, since there isn't any extra oxygen available, and since fat needs oxygen to metabolise, additional fat burning is all but turned off. The 5% of the total calories burned or so of the total energy burned in the Redline zone that is from fats isn't as helpful as in your lower zones.

For the calorie counters in the crowd, the Redline is a great zone, because you are burning the highest number of calories per minute of any of the five zones - up to 20 calories per minute depending on your weight and muscle mass. But, unfortunately, there aren't very many minutes involved in Redline training, because you are in and out of the Redline zone because you can't sustain the intensity for long.

The Redline zone is so hot that it demands the purest of fuels - the highest octanes available to get the maximum combustion and thrust out of each muscle contraction. Our body's preferred high-octane fuel is glycogen, or broken-down carbohydrates. Even if your body could use the low grade fuels, fats or fatty acids, in the Redline zone, it would be like putting diesel in your Ferrari - not recommended.

Our skeletal muscles love glucose or, as we like to think of it, "muscle sugar." Glucose, when it is burned at high-intensity heart rates, is chemically transformed into lactates which, as we know, are acids. It's the build-up of these acids which leads to acidosis, that tell-tale feeling of overall fatigue, heavily wooden limbs, hard breathing, and burning muscle pain.

REDLINING AND OVERTRAINING

If you want to get fast, you have to train fast. It's a standard rule that SSD (short slow distance) and LSD (long slow distance) workouts aren't valuable as anything but recovery workouts for the individual training for high performance. However, the Redline zone is so hot that an overdose or miscalculation in training here can result in long-term damage and the need for long-term recovery.

There are some serious consequences of hanging out too long in this zone. First, with the high levels of acidosis from the presence of lactic acid, muscle cell enzymes are affected. That is, the enzymes that are responsible for aerobic metabolism are sabotaged, and one's aerobic endurance capacity is hurt. Repeated days of high intensity redlining results in damage to these enzymes, and you simply can't train aerobically without problems.

What really happens is that the lactic acid damages the muscle cell wall. Like any wall, the damaged muscle cell wall breaks down, and the cell material leaks out into the blood. That's when you see increases in certain blood panel concentrations like urea and CPK. It means that the walls are leaking.

for your information:

The purest of the forms of glycogen is ATP, or adenosine triphosphate. When you are in the Redline Zone and sprinting a 100-yard dash, you are burning principally ATP. Here's the catch - we only have enough ATP available in storage for about 10 seconds, before it's exhausted, Clearly ATP is not a fuel to be dependent on - it burns off as fast as it takes a match to burn out.

If you don't heed the warning signs and do some training in the lower zones - or simply rest - your ability to train will continue to diminish substantially, because a cell wall takes a long time to recover.

Among the common negative outcomes of too much time in the Redline zone:

• **Interference with coordination capacity.** In sports like soccer, skiing, martial arts, basketball, and ice skating, where both endurance and coordination are requirements, there is little to no improvement in technical skills when the individual is exposed to the upper Redline zone and near exhaustion. High lactic acid contents in the blood interfere with coordination, lessening the benefits of training, not increasing them.

• **Increased red blood cell destruction rate.** Red blood cells are responsible for carrying oxygen, and their health and numerical stability in the bloodstream is obviously of vital importance to anyone, let alone the endurance athlete. Yet, when training in the Redline zone, acidosis causes the membranes of red blood cells to become unstable, which makes them more fragile. This fragility is augmented by the number of red blood cells that are destroyed because of mechanical trauma and the increased speed of the blood flow into small capillary vessels.

• **Increased risk of injuries.** High acidosis within the muscle tissues result in weakening of the muscles to such an extent that severe muscle injuries occur more readily.

• **Diminished ATP energy renewal.** Again because of the high concentration of lactic acid, ATP, the energy source for short bursts, does not reformulate as quickly. This delay in reformation severely limits one's ability to perform short sprints of exercise during training sessions.

• **Damage to aerobic capacity.** The lactic acidosis also causes damage to endurance capacity because it interferes with the various enzyme mechanisms which enhance oxygen utilisation.

All that being said, we shouldn't place *all* the blame for the Redline zone's possible ill effects on lactates. The current thinking is that there are a number of different occurrences that cumulatively prevent you from continuing to contract those muscles and move forward. One of the current suspects, generated through exercise along with lactic acids, are hydrogen ions (also known as free radical – which are cell-damaging agents, by the way). In brief, it seems that when your blood is loaded up with hydrogen ions, from high intensity exercise, the muscle pH drops (producing acidosis), and it is this drop in the pH which additionally hurts or impairs the metabolic processes that produce energy and muscle contractions. For more details on this, read Ken Cooper's book, *Antioxident Revolution*.

Z5 TRAINING HAS ITS RISKS.

Individuals who spend a lot of time training in high zones are not only taking a risk of potential overtraining from too much high intensity workloads, they are also at increased risk of impairing their immune system. As well, those who accumulate high HZT weekly points, are also at higher risk, regardless of their time in each zone. High training volume has been shown to result in a higher number of individuals who become ill from respiration and other infections.

HZT Points are a way of measuring training dosage. More details on this in Chapter 12.

It's not just the high zone or the high heart rate numbers which determine frequency of illness - it can also be one single exhausting workout. For example, in a recent study, after running a 26.2 mile marathon, 13% of the runners who completed the marathon became sick shortly after the race while only 2% of runners who trained for the same marathon but who didn't actually run it became sick. It seems that a high dose in a single day of exercise weakens the immune system as well.

High zone training can downgrade the immune system because

it results in a physiological response of the body which produces an increase in stress hormones (such as cortisol and catechol-amines). Stress hormones decrease the activity of certain immune cells (T cells and NK cells) which are responsible for directly killing virally infected cells and invading microorganisms. Your defense or your resistance against infectious agents is compromised by high zone training.

Just as you may know about the "stress-makes-you-sick" problem from psychological stress, stress makes you stupid, too. Exercise coupled with psychological stress further impairs immune function. Stress from competition, your coach, family expectations, sponsors, and spectators added to the stress of lack of sleep, travel to events, and absence from home can increase the risk of infection and may lead to sub-par performances.

Overtraining caused by high-volume and/or high intensity training with inadequate recovery results in the loss of performance. It's not reserved for competitive athletes. First timers and recreational exercisers who crank up their HZT points too high and too fast are subject to the over-training syndrome. It's usually too late when the symptoms appear, and they can literally appear "out of the blue" with little or no advance warning signs.

To calculate HZT Points, all you have to do is multiply the zone number by the number of minutes you train in that zone.

There is a way to reduce the risk if you have sophisticated and effective ways to monitor immune-cell concentrations and blood sampling, but this is expensive and not available to most. Even with an optimal fortified nutritional program, with regular recovery and rest periods, it's difficult to avoid the immune-suppressing stress hormones associated with high zone training.

REDLINE INTERVALS

Ultimately, the Redline zone is the place where you can exercise yourself into exhaustion and optimum athletic training. This high level of fatigue has always fascinated exercise scientists. In my graduate years at U.C. Berkeley, I began my research by attempting to answer the fatigue question. In my athletic years, I have trained and raced in some of the longest and hardest races in the world in a continuing attempt to understand what makes us exhausted and what we can do about it.

The personal reason I want to find the source of fatigue is to combat it - to override it so we can go further and faster. It's a truism that love-hate relationships are the most dangerous. You thirst for the love and suffer from the hate, and together the ambivalence can drive you crazy. For me (and others!) the Redline zone is exactly that same relationship. You thirst for the benefits (enhanced performance) and suffer from the experience (pain), and together they can drive you to stardom or failure.

Still, because it is difficult, if not downright dangerous, to hang out for any length of time in the Redline zone, it is time that needs to be carefully planned. We stay there for a short time, then recover and hop back into it. Then it's out to rest again. This is called interval training, and there are actually two types of intervals: the exercise interval and the rest interval. The exercise or training interval is the amount of time that we spend at a certain heart rate or workload. The rest interval is the time that we spend recovering from the exercise interval.

For example, let's say you want to do lower Redline zone intervals (90–95% Max HR). You could do short, or "sprint" intervals (rather than middle or long intervals) of one minute at that heart rate, with a one-minute active recovery interval. That's called a 1:1 ratio of effort to rest, because you are spending equal amounts of time (a minute each, in this case) exercising and resting.

Z5 Redline Zone 90% - 100% Maximum Heart Rate Chart

Max HR	150	155	160	165	170	175	180	185	190	195	200	205	210 bpm
90%		135	140	144	149	153	158	162	167	171	176	180	184	189
100%		150	155	160	165	170	175	180	185	190	195	200	205	210

If your Max HR were 200 bpm, then to do this lower Redline workout you would exercise in a narrow zone of 180-190 bpm for one minute. Then you'd slow considerably and rest, still moving (this is an *active* rest), letting your heart rate drop for one minute. Each group of one minute in Z5 and one minute out of Redline is the "interval set." You may choose to do 6-10 of these sets for your workout.

This Redline workout can be done on a track, on a bike, nordic skiing, running, or swimming.

In your monitor, set the upper zone to 95% of your true Max HR. In the case of someone whose Max HR is 200, they would set the monitor to 190 beats per minute. Next set the monitor's alarm to sound at every one minute. Use an active recovery of 30-60 seconds by walking, gliding or slow pedalling before you begin the next interval. Break the workout into two sets of five different 1:1 interval repeats, with a 3-5 minute rest between each set.

The reason you want active recovery between the exercise interval is to sustain high levels of lactates in your blood. That's one of the main purposes of the workout - lactate tolerance training. You are trying to build up your lactate concentrations during the session. When there is too much recovery, your lactates drop. If you can't finish 5 repeats the first couple of tries, that's fine. Start with 2-4 and build your way up.

There is a slight delay between your real heart rate and the monitor reading. That's because your heart rate is higher than the monitor because it is updating the data each 5 seconds, so it is always delayed - on both the active and the recovery times. This lagging of your monitor behind your true heart rate is one of the drawbacks to the technology as it exists today. In the near future there will be real-time heart rate monitors. But for now be satisfied that the data is so close (far better than you could derive from taking your pulse) and remember that we are only listening for the alarm as we accelerate our heart rate into the Redline zone.

For runners who like track workouts, two of my favourites are called ladders and "dropping 1 second per quarter." Both add new dimensions to an already overtaxing experience. With ladders, change the heart rate ceiling by 2 beats (or 1%) per lap.

In our example, the first lap is 190 bpm, second is 192, third is 194 until the fifth lap and then go back down the ladder. The second variation is to use time as the stimulus. Drop one second in time for each quarter for the last five quarters.

This is truly a delayed gratification workout. Tomorrow you will be tired and sore and wonder why - you're thinking just a few laps around the track in the Redline zone shouldn't fatigue you to this extent. But it does! All Redline training sessions will cheerily work you to the max. Only if you allow yourself recovery time can you arise as a stronger and faster athlete.

HEART RATE IN THE ANIMAL KINGDOM

(From W.S. Spector, *Handbook of Biology*, 1956.)

Animal	Average Heart Rate (bpm)	Heart Rate Range (bpm)
Camel	30	25-32
Elephant	35	22-53
Lion	40	N/A
Horse	44	23-70
Ass	50	40-56
Human	**70**	**58-104**
Giraffe	66	N/A
Sheep	75	60-120
Cat	120	110-140
Dog	N/A	100-130
Rabbit	205	123-304
Squirrel	249	96-378
Rat	328	261-600
Hamster	450	300-600
Mouse	534	324-858

Workout #7:
REDLINE WORKOUT: TEN MAX QUARTERS

Introduction. This is one of those track workouts which can be used for different sports - cycling, nordic skiing or running. Even swimmers can do 200s and the workout is the same. When you are performing it, you have one of those contradictory experiences. You wonder is it the leg burn that hurts or is it my lungs from breathing so hard?

Metal to the floor! That's what the Redline training is all about. If you have that masochistic sense of feeling it in every cell, here's where you will be in your own element. It's best to do this workout with some fellow lactic hedonists as you can push yourself even harder.

Purpose. The purpose of the workout is lactate tolerance training. You are trying to build up your lactate concentrations during the session by exercising in the Redline zone or 90-100 percent of maximum heart rate (Max HR).

Workout Plan. This track workout is a series of 10 quarter-mile repeats performed at 90-95 percent of your true Max HR. For someone with a Max HR rate of 200, this number would be 180-190 bpm. The workout is broken into two sets of five quarters with a short recovery between quarters and a longer rest between sets.

Workout. Set the ceiling or upper limit of your monitor to signal at 95 percent of Max HR. A lower limit will not be necessary. After a warm up, cycle, ski or run hard for your first quarter mile (or 200 yards, if swimming). The goal is to set off your alarm before you reach the end of the quarter. Use an active recovery by jogging, skiing or pedalling slowly until your heart rate breaks through the 70% of max rate then start with the next quarter. Take a 3-5 minute rest after the first set of five quarters and then do a second set.

If 10 quarters are too difficult in the beginning, start with five and build your way up. Be sure to keep your recovery active to sustain the level of lactates in your blood. You are trying to increase your lactate concentration and too much recovery will allow your lactates to drop.

Recognise that your HR is actually higher than displayed because the monitor is updating the data every few seconds and running the information through a series of mathematical equations called algorithms. This lag behind true-time HR is one of the drawbacks of monitor technology as it exists today. The data will be close enough so just listen for the alarm as you accelerate into the Redline zone.

Comment. This is truly a workout which offers delayed gratification. Tomorrow you may be tired and sore. You'll also wonder why just a few laps around the track in the Redline zone are so fatiguing. All lactate tolerance training sessions stress you to the max as they also build you up.

Heart Zone
Training Points

Thanks to Ken Cooper, MD, writing the paradigm-shifting book *Aerobics* almost thirty years ago, the world has taken a giant step forward by following his exercise prescription of counting "aerobic points". He carefully designed a new generation of exercise and sparked a revolution in fitness that was based on important principles, including self-testing, measurement tools to manage your workouts, and a quantification method to reward exercise outcomes - the Aerobic Point System.

I was an undergraduate student at UC Berkeley's Physical Education department when Cooper, then a young Air Force officer and physician came to campus and lectured on the principles of aerobic training. Those same principles have stayed with me and allowed me to better appreciate what's needed for high performance training and racing.

The Heart Zone Training Point System is truly one of the first high performance athlete, coach and trainer systems that has allowed to quantify workload. This is truly a pivotal step which can take you to an entirely new level of training and performing.

Training Load is the quantity of exercise stress as measured by the F.I.T. formula of frequency, intensity and time (or duration). If you were to multiply these three parameters of an exercise bout, you would have a measurement of total workload also known as dosage. Now, with the HZT Point System, there is a way to calculate these three variables.

The formula is as follows:

Frequency x Intensity x Time = Training Load

The missing piece in this formula which has prevented the measurement of exercise workload and eluded and frustrated us for all of these years is the "I" for intensity. A heart rate monitor measures exercise intensity. Only now, with the use of this piece of fitness hardware can we measure workload.

The HZT Point System uses the quantification of frequency as number of workouts per week, intensity as measured by numerical heart zones, and time as the amount of time in each zone to determine daily, weekly, and monthly points.

The first step to determine your HZT points is to use heart zones. If you spend twenty minutes a day in zone three that workout is valued at 60 points which is 20 x 3. If you did that workout for four days, which meets the ACSM Guidelines for minimum exercise, you'd discover that you'd earn 240 points, the minimum number of points needed to obtain the minimum exercise requirement.

ACSM Guidelines

3 days x Z3 x 20 minutes = 240 Points   4 days x Z3 x 30 minutes = 360 Points

It appears that to meet the requirements set by the American College of Sports Medicine, you would need to get about 300 points a week to meet the minimum standards.

What's the maximum number of points? What's a healthy number of points? What's the ideal number of points? What's the best number of points you need to set a PR (personal record) in a race?

Here's the incredible news. We can now, using the HZT Point System and the Variability Index or, V.I., predict when you will be at your peak performance level. You can now know when you are training towards the point of injury or over-training or when you are at high probability for a breakdown - mental or physical. That's because each person has an individual **training load threshold** or a quantifiable amount of exercise that they can sustain which allows them to achieve peak performance.

If you are wondering how, the answer is that your training load threshold is a certain range or number of HZT points. You may have a threshold of 4,000 points per week and someone else may have a workload threshold of 1,000 points. It doesn't mean you're a better athlete, faster, or fitter but that your tolerance of exercise quantity is higher than mine. I may have a more sensitive immune system than yours or you may have an injury that, after a certain amount of stress, just says it's enough or you will re-injure yourself. The workload threshold for exercise varies widely among individual athletes. It's your responsibility to train at different weekly point levels to determine just how much, how hard, how long you can exercise to reach high performance and your goals.

VARIABILITY INDEX (VI)

Read on if you are interested in the most advanced concepts of applied sports training systems. This information is directed towards coaches, high performance athletes, researchers and such. It's technical. Just skip this section and don't get bogged down in this level of information if you don't want to.

Variability in training has been shown to be one of the most significant parameters to successful high performance improvement. Variability means changes in the workload within a training cycle. A training cycle is a certain number of days of training which usually is a period between 7 and 21 days. In coaching lingo, it's called a mesocycle (see Glossary for definitions of macrocycles and microcycles).

Changing the frequency, intensity and time- the FIT formula is one of the most important exercise stressors. It results in training adaptation and, hence, improvement. This improved fitness occurs because changing your FIT creates a stress-recovery adaptation leading to a higher fitness level and higher work capacity or exercise capability. In other words, if you want to swim, bike, skate, run faster and stronger, progressive variability must occur in your training regimen.

Progressive variability can be measured and monitored.

Progressive variability is periodisation.

Training Variability is changing the number of HZT points day to day. Progressive training means changing the total HZT points from week to week.

Variability indexing is how we measure the amount of training variability within the same week. VI means that each week you change your HZT points, in a progressive and variable way during the week. Within each week vary your HZT points systematically increasing them until, at some point, you reach your workload threshold.

The graph below demonstrates a typical VI within a single week:

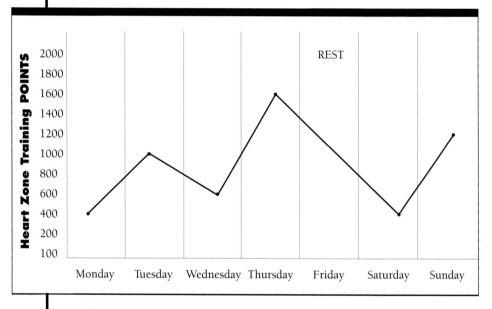

The graph on page 128 shows high VI for weekly training, which is what you are trying to achieve.

Why do you want high variability within the weekly schedule? *Answer: It provides for the stress-adaptation response to occur.*

Thanks to Karl Foster, Ph.D., author of *Physiological Assessment* and director of the Milwaukee Heart Institute, and his work with high performance athletes in particular speed skaters (many of whom live in Milwaukee which is the headquarters for their sport), "I can almost accurately predict

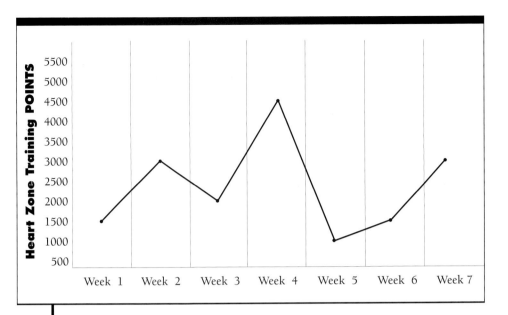

when an athlete, almost any athlete will breakdown. Here's how. I take their logbook, calculate their HZT points and then I know their workload. Next, I plot that value along with their racing performances, injuries, illness over a year period of time and can then determine quantitatively their individual workload threshold value. When they surpass their workload threshold for a relative period of time - Kaboom, they are hurt, drained, destroyed, fried, trashed."

According to Foster, for recreational runners and skaters, that individual workload value is about 2,000 HZT points per week. Working with some of the US Olympic speed skaters he has seen them reach thresholds of 6,000 HZT points and sustain it without injury. For many elite level performers, the 3,000 point threshold seems to be about the norm.

This is an area of high performance training that begs for longitudinal research. Why can some athletes get overtrained at 2,000 points and others at 6,000? Do different sports tolerate different threshold values? You are invited to be an experiment of one – use your log over the last year and plot the points. You'll probably have to guess at the I, or intensity level, but you should have the time and the frequency. Then, calculate your VI and maintain a high weekly and monthly variability that is planned and scheduled out.

Workout #8:
THE 5 BY 5 WORKOUT

Introduction. There are a few classic heart training workouts in my standard weekly sessions. I do this one, the "Five by Fiver," every Thursday morning because it fits within the 48-hour Rule: Rest 48 hours before your next Threshold (AT HR) Zone or higher workout.

Purpose. To teach your running-specific metabolic systems to adapt to constantly increasing training load every five minutes, which trains both your cardiovascular ability as well as your lactate clearance systems.

Workout Plan. Simply, this is a five-beat ladder every five minutes. Subtract 20 beats from your maximum heart rate (Max HR) to determine the top rung on your ladder and subtract 50 beats from your Max HR for your HR starting point or the first rung on the ladder. The range between these two numbers if your training zone for the "Five by Fiver."

Example: 195 (Max HR) - 20 = 175 (ceiling or top rung). 195 (Max HR) - 50 = 145 (starting point or first rung). Training zone for workout = 145-175 beats per minute (bpm).

Workout. For a warm-up, gradually increase from a walk to a slow jog to the starting point for the first five minutes. Begin the main set ladder by moving into a new five-beat every five minutes as shown in the example on the following page.

Minutes	HR Zone
0-5	Warm-up
5-10	145-150 bpm
10-15	150-155 bpm
15-20	155-160 bpm
20-25	160-165 bpm
25-30	165-170 bpm
30-35	170-175 bpm

Total Workout = 35 minutes at 145-175 bpm

Recommendation. I recommend that you start by only going up the ladder. When you are in great shape, try going up only twice in a workout. The up and then downs are really hard.

Quite honestly, this is one of my very favourite training workouts because I work myself through all of the different zones - Temperate, Aerobic and pierce into and then train to the top of my Threshold Zone. Log it as a 10-pointer for difficulty. It's a challenge but guaranteed to get you faster, stronger, and fitter!

The 10 Step Program

For years, John Lehrer, one of my favourite training partners, and I worked side by side. Together we ran 100-mile races and spread the word on training and fitness (he as a magazine editor and journalist, I as a fitness writer). Then he moved to Southern California, and we saw less and less of each other. My annual holiday letter went unanswered, and we seemed to be on the verge of completely losing touch.

So, knowing I was going to be giving a seminar on Heart Zone Training in Los Angeles, I invited him to attend as my guest. The man who appeared was twice the size I had known before. On his 150-pound frame he had added 100 pounds of fatty tissue; his energy was low and he was embarrassed to see me. "Sally, I dropped you as a friend because I didn't want you to know how I'd let myself go," he confessed.

After three hours of the seminar, buying a heart rate monitor, and starting a Heart Zone Training program, John is slowly losing fat and putting his fitness life back together again. I think he is living proof of two things: One, that loss of fitness can happen to anyone, even a former ultra-marathoner. And, two, that Heart Zone Training works.

Mix and practice this recipe, continuing to "kaizen" the program, for a lifetime.

A LIFETIME JOURNEY BEGINS WITH 10 STEPS

There are many ways of preparing your Heart Zone Training program. One of the best is what's called the Ten Steps and here they are:

A LIFETIME JOURNEY BEGINS WITH 10 STEPS

1. Determine your maximum heart rate.

2. Calculate and set your five heart zones.

3. Decide and write down your fitness goals.

4. Determine your current Training Tree Branch.

5. Determine your weekly training time in minutes.

6. Calculate your time in zone based on the Training Tree Branch

7. Fill out the Heart Zone Training (HZT) Planner.

8. Do the workout as planned.

9. Keep a log of each workout.

10. Complete monthly self tests.

"Kaizen" is a Japanese expression for constant small improvements. In other words, the Japanese see value in a program that makes a 1% improvement 100 times, resulting in more than a 100% improvement (due to the compounding effect). The American way is to make a one-time change of 100%. Which do you think has the greater chance for success? The Heart Zone Training program uses kaizen as one of its principles. After the first week on Heart Zone Training, take your pencil and make some small changes - fine-tune it. On the days where there were interruptions to your planned schedule, determine why you didn't accomplish your workout that day. Your goal is to match your planned workouts and your actual workouts so that they are mirrors of each other, exact reflections. When you write down your plan and follow it, you are going to feel an incredible sense of success and know that each day you are making a minimum 1% improvement in your fitness life.

STEP 1.

Determine your maximum heart rate.

Max Heart Rate: _____ bpm

STEP 2.

Calculate and set your five heart zones.

Heart Zone	# Beats per Minute
100% Max HR	_____ bpm
90% Max HR	_____ bpm
80% Max HR	_____ bpm
70% Max HR	_____ bpm
60% Max HR	_____ bpm
50% Max HR	_____ bpm

STEP 3.

Decide and write down your fitness goals.

Training Goal 1:_____

_____

_____

_____

Date to be Accomplished:_____

Training Goal 2:_____

_____

_____

_____

Date to be Accomplished:_____

STEP 4.

Determine your current branch on The Training Tree. Let's stop here and study the Training Tree.

THE TRAINING TREE

When you're ready to assemble all of these parts - your goals, heart rate zones and points, and your exercise time - into a cohesive and integrated program, remember that like snowflakes, flowers, or redwoods, no two training programs are alike. I like to look at my training program as a tree with many branches, each of them lifting me higher, yet remaining there, solid as ever, when I want to pull back on the intensity of my experience and climb down a little.

The training tree starts at the bottom, with its roots. The roots of the tree are information and education, thirsting for the water of learning and nearly as large below the ground as the branches are above. The branches are at different levels and each must be scaled to reach the tree top, which holds your goal. As you start to create your own personalised training tree, always focus on the top limb, as that is what drives all of the parts or branches in the training system.

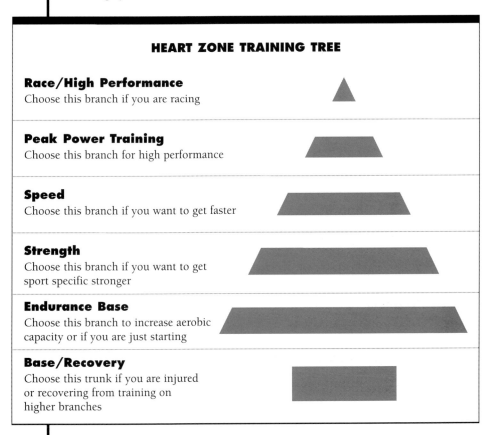

HEART ZONE TRAINING TREE

Race/High Performance
Choose this branch if you are racing

Peak Power Training
Choose this branch for high performance

Speed
Choose this branch if you want to get faster

Strength
Choose this branch if you want to get
sport specific stronger

Endurance Base
Choose this branch to increase aerobic
capacity or if you are just starting

Base/Recovery
Choose this trunk if you are injured
or recovering from training on
higher branches

BRANCH 1: ENDURANCE BRANCH

This is the starting point of any training program. Base training is slow, easy, fun. It is the lower three zones; endurance training is the same as basic training. The purpose of spending time in the first branch is to develop your cardiovascular endurance to the point that you can easily sustain a workout without a great deal of fatigue and muscle soreness. The base endurance branch is a great place to hang out because it's so easy and relaxing with no pressure – just simply time in the low zones.

EXERCISE PHYSIOLOGY OF BRANCH 1

Adaptation	Explanation	Information
• Improved VO_2	VO2 is the volume of oxygen that you can consume in one minute	Because your lung, heart, and skeletal muscles are in better condition you can deliver more oxygen to the muscles
• Movement Efficiency	Balance, coordination, proficiency	As you do a specific movement, you develop more motor coordination so you can go farther on less energy.
• Enhanced Fat Burning	You become a better fat burner	Increased amount of movement increases the amount of calories that you burn. And at low intensity you burn a higher percentage and a higher total number of fat calories.
• Joint System Stronger	Ligaments and tendons that connect bones, muscles, and joints become more capable of securing you during weight bearing activity.	Ligaments and tendons thicken in the adaptation process as the strain of weight bearing activity requires them to become stronger. You may become less flexible which is why stretching exercises become important to maintain your range of motion.
• Psychological Patience	With longer workout time some people say they experience boredom from exercise.	By slowly building your exercise time you become accustomed to working gently for longer time without getting mentally stale.
• Improved stamina	Your ability to sustain longer periods of exercise at a sub maximal workload	Aerobic endurance is the starting point for fitness because it allows you to sustain an increased amount of exercise dosage until it begins to feel easy which is when it's time to move up the HZT Training Tree.

Frequency per week: 3-5 workouts *
Time: 15-30 minutes per workout**
Period: 2-4 weeks
Heart Zones: Z1 through Z3
Benefits: Comfortable, sustained, steady-state exercise

There's a reason to hang out on each of the branches and that's because while you are spending time on the branch change occurs. In exercise science this change is referred to as "adaptation". Adaptation is a response process in which change occurs. On each of the five different branches, there is a different response because as the stress increases, the adaptation to that stress occurs. As you progress through each of the branches look for the explanation of the physiological changes which occur. The explanation on the previous page – Exercise Physiology of Branch 1 - should help you to understand this better.

BRANCH 2: STRENGTH BRANCH

It's time to add that all-important exercise stimulus: resistance training. Following many of the same principles that weight lifters use, athletes stimulate muscle power by applying appropriate resistance stimuli to the specific activity that they are training for. That is, it is known that if you "overload" the specific muscle by repeatedly asking it to work at higher levels of workload, usually at a slower rate, the muscle responds by getting stronger. Favourite examples of resistance training are stairs - use office buildings, bleachers, stair machines at the club or hill intervals. Find a few rolling hills - mountains will do - and work the uphills in Z3. The downhills are active resting in the Z2 zone. The benefits are enormous. The ability to climb hills is a specific stimulus that leads to increased speed and strength.

Frequency: 2 workouts per week of strength +3 workouts of endurance
Time: 20-60 minutes
Period: 3-4 weeks

Heart Zones: Z2 through Z3
Benefits: Sport-specific muscle strength

The strength branch is a time for more than just doing strength resistance training with weights and machines. Sure they are important. Since a lot of lower body weight training is in the seated position, it isolates different muscles than when you are standing. Further, you aren't required to support your body weight during seated repetitions. As a result, your specific lower body muscles do get generally stronger and they become adept at exerting power while you are sitting down. It's then important to take this improvement in general strength to the specific muscle strength required by that sport activity.

Most weight training routines focus on individual joints and muscles and don't require your muscles to support full body weight. That's why training on hills or in the water with resistance devices builds more sports specific strength. For example, running *up hills* forces the muscles in all parts of your leg - from your hips, legs, ankles and feet to exert power while fully supporting your body weight. Hill workouts stress the lower leg muscles resulting in dramatic increases in running power. With more power, you get the benefits of longer, faster running strides.

Take the Kenyan runners for an example. They are some of the best runners in the world, in spite of the fact that they never go to a gym and lift weights. Their "gym" consists of the hills and mountains of their rugged homeland and upon their daily training regimen.

Research supports what runners have known for a long time about hill running. Bengt Saltin, Ph. D. has examined the muscle tissue of hill runners and found they have higher concentrations of "aerobic enzymes" (those are the chemicals which help muscles to consume oxygen at higher heart rates for longer periods of time without fatigue) than the muscles of the runners who only train on flat ground.

To improve your leg-muscle power, to enhance your sport-specific economy, to protect your legs against soreness and, in running, to increase stride length, the strength branch of the tree

EXERCISE PHYSIOLOGY OF BRANCH 2

Adaptation	Explanation	Information
• Improved VO_2	The volume of oxygen burned per pound of body weight per minute increases, which is good.	You are training more time in higher zones which means more intensity. As you train at higher heart rates you burn higher amounts of oxygen per minute.
• Movement Efficiency	More distance per calorie expended. (As in a car getting higher miles per gallon.)	You are now moving faster, which requires more coordination than in lower branches.
• Enhanced Fat Burning	Changes in the blend of fuels burned, which is the ratio of carbohydrate (CHO) to fat.	You are burning more total fat calories and, since you are training in the lower three or Fat Burning Zones, you are burning more total calories. You'll also be burning more fat when you are at rest than before.
• Joint System Stronger	Thickening of the connective tissues that hold joints together.	Tendons connect muscles to muscles. Ligaments connect muscles to bones. Both are part of the support system of every joint. By getting thicker they get tighter so you have a more secure joint.
• Psychological Patience	Exercise intensity is increasing but time in zone is staying the same so your patience now begins to shift to the feeling that results from higher heart rates.	At higher heart rates you are breathing harder and will feel the intensity as an expression of less comfort in the sport specific muscles and harder breathing.
• Improved endurance stamina	Aerobic endurance is extended.	You'll be able to go further, faster, longer, easier because you have become more efficient and your ability to sustain work longer and longer improves.

is the place to hang out. The most common kind of strength training session is called "hill training". There are two different basic kinds of hill workouts. To boost your leg-muscle power, one of the best methods is find a very steep slope at least 25 meters from the bottom to the top.

The second way of optimally improving your performance during this stage of strength training is to increase the aerobic capabilities and to improve the fatigue resistance of your muscles is by finding a "set" of hills that are moderate in nature and which you can train over for 20-30 minutes. Find a hilly park or a bunch of sand dunes along the shore or rolling terrain in the country and use them for this workout. You'll do your recovery phase as you saunter down the backside and your high intensity phase as you work your way to the top of Z4 and hopefully, on your recovery back into Z2.

BRANCH 3: SPEED

If you want to race fast, train fast and train strong. This is the phase that builds upon the lower three branches by adding your first Redline workouts with short or endurance intervals. It's the branch where you start time trials at specific heart rate points to test improvement. It's the period of seeing big heart rate numbers, because you are pushing towards your Max HR. It's time to watch for the highest sustainable heart rate and to work at raising that value. For cyclists, it's time to breathe hard and stare at the monitor as you push yourself and your monitor to new dimensions. This is interval training - specific interval training that matches your racing or performance goals. If you are a sprinter, then long intervals are not going to be of as much value. Use a variety of interval training regimens and workload ratios during this phase

Frequency: 2-3 workouts plus endurance and strength workouts
Time: 20-60 minutes
Period: 3-4 weeks
Heart Zones: Z3 through Z5
Benefits: Improved speed, lactic acid removal and glucose fuel utilisation.

EXERCISE PHYSIOLOGY OF BRANCH 3. SPEED

Adaptation	Explanation	Information
• Improved VO_2	Your ability to transport oxygen into the muscle and carbon dioxide out of the muscle greatly improves.	This is the phase of training when you go beyond an RQ or respiratory quotient of 1.0, which is the anaerobic threshold, when more carbon dioxide is produced than oxygen can be delivered, so you shift into oxygen debt stage or anaerobic metabolism.
• Lactate Tolerance	Lactic acid is a byproduct of energy metabolism.	When lactic acid is produced because of insufficient oxygen present, it needs to be shuttled out of the muscle to be resynthesized. The amount of lactic acid as measured in pH or acidosis levels is called your lactic tolerance buffering ability.
• Improved Biomechanics	Like efficiency, this is enhancement of your structural alignment and enhanced coordination	When your biomechanics improve so does your ability to move the same distance in the same time at a lower heart rate reading. That's truly the outcome of improved efficiency and biomechanics.
• Enhanced Glucose and Fat Burning	You become a better fat burner and a better carbohydrate (CHO) burner.	You are burning higher amounts of both fat and CHO because you need more of the easy to burn CHO for higher intensity training.
• Joint System Stronger	Ligaments and tendons that connect bones, muscles, and joints become more capable of securing you during weight bearing activity.	Ligaments and tendons thicken in the adaptation process as the strain of weight bearing activity requires them to become stronger. You may become less flexible which is why stretching exercises become important to maintain your range of motion.

continued next page

EXERCISE PHYSIOLOGY OF BRANCH 3. SPEED CONTINUED

Adaptation	Explanation	Information
• Psychological Patience	With longer workout time some may experience boredom from exercise.	By slowly building your exercise time, you become accustomed to working gently for a longer time without getting mentally stale. Diversify training partners and mode of exercise.
• Change in Muscle Fibre Recruitment	There are two types of muscle fibres: fast twitch and slow twitch.	During this phase more fast twitch Type II muscle fibres are required such that they are converted to look and behave more like slow twitch fibres which are the ones needed.
• Economy	Improvement in stride length, capillary bed build-up, all around efficiency of movement.	Like in a car, it's you getting the most miles per gallon because you are so efficient in your biomechanics, oxygen uptake, muscle recruitment, and it's demonstrated by your ability to hold pace over the entire distance of a race.

BRANCH 4: PEAK

This period of training is a favourite for many athletes. The peaking phase is the time when you put all of the other branches together into one: endurance, strength, and intervals. It is the variety branch. It is the time when you are incredibly fit and loving it. It's the time when you get to experience all of the heart zones. It's a precision training period. It's high intensity, it's resistance training, it's growing endurance, it's recovery workouts, it's incredibly challenging. And through all of it, it is a period of listening to your body, because it's during these weeks that overtraining most frequently occurs.

EXERCISE PHYSIOLOGY OF BRANCH 4. PEAK

Adaptation	Explanation	Information
• Improved VO_2	As you train at higher intensities for longer periods of time you can increase your Max VO_2 levels. This is how you train your stamina.	Your Max VO_2 continues to improve until you reach a point that is your sport specific and genetic maximum amount, after which additional training will no longer improve your oxygen carrying capacity.
• Lactate Tolerance	Like VO_2, as you train your ability to tolerate higher concentrations of lactic acid increase. This branch is called "lactic acid land" because you will be spewing the stuff out of your muscles.	Like VO_2, there is a limit to the amount of acidosis or lactic acid that you can buffer at any one point. You will reach your highest value and then no longer improve. If you overtrain, however, this tolerance level is compromised.
• Improved Biomechanics	During this phase you are training all three building blocks:endurance, speed, strength.	The power branch is the most important because you are training at your hardest and driving all four systems: muscle contraction speed (intervals), aerobic and anaerobic endurance (stamina), and muscle strength (ability of muscle to contract under higher loads).
• Enhanced Glucose and Fat Burning	As measured in calories per minute, this is the peak number of calories burned during any of the branches.	Because of higher heart rate levels and workload levels, you are burning the highest amount of fat and highest amount of carbohydrates (CHO) of any of the branches.
• Joint System Stressed	This is a time to beware of connective tissue problems.	With high workloads and intensities come the potential for tendon problems or joint stress or ligament complications. Listen to your body's pain levels and stress.

continued next page

EXERCISE PHYSIOLOGY OF BRANCH 4. PEAK CONTINUED

Adaptation	Explanation	Information
• Psychological Intensity	It's a high limb on the tree and high psychological intensity comes with it.	Staleness can come from more than just physiological stress. It can also result from the mental toughness needed to grit your teeth through increasingly harder workouts.
• Economy	You are at the top of your sport specific training period and you might feel the stress of all out training.	Note that you might see a decreased appetite, both in your libido and your dietary appetites. If you don't stretch, you'll notice a certain lack of range of motion in your joints. Maintain flexibility during this period.

Frequency: 6-7 workouts (e.g: 2 endurance, 2 interval, 2 strength, 1 recovery)
Time: 30-120+ minutes
Period: 2 weeks through entire season
Heart Zones: All
Benefits: Putting it all together to optimise high-performance fitness

BRANCH 5: RACING

Racing is a very tenacious branch. It's as much psychological as it is physical. The demands are arduous because it requires constant testing, usually against other athletes as well as against your own goals and that great truth-teller - the clock. It requires constant recuperation and resting, too. I've been asked more times than I can remember which I prefer - training or racing. I always answer that training is like eating cake, but the racing is adding the ice cream, and I love the two together. Racing is my favourite branch because it challenges so much more than just my body. It requires toeing up to the line and testing yourself against yourself, because that is who the race in life is really with. But it also requires the ability to cut back after the race, to recover, to regain speed and power and strength and endurance to race again.

Frequency: If racing: 4 workouts. If not racing that week: 6-7 workouts
Time: 30-120+ minutes
Period: up to 12 weeks
Heart Zones: All
Benefits: To successfully race throughout a season without injury or staleness.

EXERCISE PHYSIOLOGY OF BRANCH 5. RACING

Adaptation	Explanation	Information
• Improved VO_2	You are there. It happened in the Power Branch, not now.	Your goal here is to maintain the high level of training that got you here. You are trying to make sure that your fitness does not diminish, and frequent testing is advised to measure this.
• Lactate Tolerance	You are here. Your anaerobic threshold heart rate should be at its highest number.	This is a time you want to go into an exercise lab and have your VO_2 and lactic acids measured so you have some information, because "you can only manage what you can measure and monitor" - one of our five principles.
• Biomechanical Efficiency	Because you are trying to hold a high physiological training level, it's a great time to work on improving your movement efficiency.	Continue to concentrate on moving smoothly, effortlessly, in a way such that you feel like you can get into "the flow"- a physiological state during training where it feels as if time has no dimension or responsibility.
• Enhanced Glucose and Fat Burning	You need to maintain efficient fat and CHO burning ability.	Since muscles are fuelled by high octane fuels that are carried in high octane blood, eat a balanced and high carbohydrate diet.
• Joint System Stronger	Propensity towards skeletal injuries.	During any high performance phase of training, there is a higher risk of breakdown from both skeletal as well as immunity compromises.
• Psychological State	Varies tremendously among individuals.	For many, this is the best of all times on the training tree and for others it's the most psychologically stressful.
• Economy	Balance of all parts of life is the key to reaching high economic state.	Look to keep all parts together: social, family, emotional, spiritual, financial, and job responsibilities, as well as physical well being.

RECOVERY: THE TRUNK, NOT A BRANCH.

Recovery period is one of the least understood and appreciated parts of the training tree, yet it is a critical part of your training phases or periods. The recovery period does not consist of "junk workouts" or time just spent in a low zone. Rather, it is a period in your annual training schedule when it is time to take a break while still maintaining fitness. Some athletes choose to develop a training plan with a recovery period in the "off season." In this cycling of workouts, a recovery period is critical to allow the body a long period of rest-up to 4-8 weeks-to recover from the rigors of high-intensity training regimens. All recovery workouts are in the two lower zones with an infrequent lower Aerobic zone workout. The benefit is recuperative in all ways from intramuscular to emotional rest.

Frequency: 4-6
Duration: 15 minutes - 1 hour
Period: 4 weeks - 3 months
Heart Zones: Healthy Heart, Temperate, Lower Aerobic
Benefits: Rest and to regain energy

HEART ZONE TRAINING TREE CHART

Maximum Heart Rate (beats/min)	Base/Recovery	Endurance	Strength	Speed/Interval	Peak
Z5 Red Line 90-100% of Max.	-	-	-	6 mins	6 mins
Z4 Threshold 80-90% of Max.	-	-	6 mins	6 mins	12 mins
Z3 Aerobic 70-80% of Max.	-	30 mins	42 mins	36 mins	36 mins
Z2 Temperate 60-70% of Max.	42 mins	24 mins	6 mins	12 mins	6 mins
Z1 Healthy Heart 60-70% of Max.	18 mins	6 mins	6 mins	-	-

• Time in Zone for 1 Hour Session

STEP 5. Determine your weekly training time in minutes.

How many days per week? _____ days per week

How many minutes per day?_____ minutes per day

How many minutes per week?_____ minutes per week

TIME IN ZONE

Developing a training program that fits into the training tree depends on you and your schedule and commitments. It must be in written form, and it's best to post it. Old paradigm training programs are usually written using the measurement controls of distance or speed - it's a 50-mile running week or a 10,000-yard swim week. Your new paradigm training program works with the time in zone (TIZ) plan, so the workouts are written in time and in zone, not distance.

Time in zone starts with determining how much time you can commit to your high performance program. Then, develop the plan around that amount of time.

Let's use the example of someone who has seven hours a week available for training. Dividing that by seven days to get a daily value, we find that this athlete has one hour per day to train. This means that a typical workout could encompass a range from 45 to 90 minutes. This individual is a single-sport athlete, with five years of training and racing experience, and is training for a half-marathon. Here's an example to be used by you only as a guideline of what a weekly workout looks like.

Determine your weekly training schedule by starting with the amount of time available and multiply it according to the percentages given for each training branch. The percentages depend on the training tree limb that you are currently scaling. To fine tune your program, adjust it based on the specific sport and event that you are training for.

After determining the number of minutes you have available for the week, divide these minutes into their respective zones. Then, plug the minutes into a weekly schedule. For example, let's continue with the 420 minutes per week - an hour a day -

SAMPLE HEART ZONE TRAINING WORKOUT PLAN

Time: 420 minutes (7 hours per week)

Branch: Peaking

Goal: 90-minute finish time for a half marathon with the race in 4 weeks

Daily Average Time: 1 hour

Range: .75 to 1.5 hours   **Max HR:** 200

	Time	Zone	Zone #	Type	HZT Points
M	60 min	Aerobic	Z3	Continuous run at 150 bpm Stretching for 1/2 hour	180
T	45 min	Redline	Z5	9 x 5 min at 180-190 bpm	225
W	60 min	Temperate or	Z2	Recovery: slow and easy Complete Rest Day	120
Th	60 min	Threshold	Z4	Hill intervals	240
F	60 min	Lower Aerobic	Z3	Cross Train: bike, swim, ski, snow shoe, circuit train, skate	180
S	45 min	Threshold	Z4	Continuous at race heart rate pace or… Highest sustainable heart rate pace 10 K fun run or race	180
S	90 min	Aerobic	Z3	Endurance Day	270

Summary of Week

Total Time: 7 hours	Time in Zones:	1 Temperate workout	60 min. /14%
Total HZT Points: 1,375		3 Aerobic workouts	210 min./50%
		2 Threshold workouts	105 min./25%
		1 Redline workout	45 min./11%
			420 min./100%

high-performance trainer. Here's what this individual's percentage of training time by zone resembles:

STEP 6. Calculate your time in zone based on the Training Tree Branch

TIME IN ZONE

Zone	Max HR	Zone	Endurance		Strength		Speed		Peak	
Z5	90–100%	Redline	---		---		10%		10%	
Z4	80–90%	Threshold	---		10%		10%		20%	
Z3	70–80%	Aerobic	10%		70%		60%		60%	
Z2	60–70%	Temperate	80%		10%		10%		10%	
Z1	50–60%	Healthy Heart	10%		10%		10%		---	
			100%	Min.	100%	Min.	100%	Min.	100%	Min.

STEP 7. Fill out the Heart Zone Training (HZT) Planner.

Day	Date	Sport/Activity	Time in Zones					Daily Points
			Z1	Z2	Z3	Z4	Z5	
Mon								
Tues								
Wed								
Thurs								
Fri								
Sat								
Sun								

Zone Name:	Zone Points	% of Max HR
Redline Zone	5	100-90%
Threshold Zone	4	90-80%
Aerobic Zone	3	80-70%
Temperate Zone	2	70-60%
Healthy Heart Zone	1	60-50%

Z1	Z2	Z3	Z4	Z5	Weekly HZT Points Total
					% TIZ

Total Weekly HZT Points: Multiply the time in each zone by the number of that zone.

STEP 8. Do the workout as planned.

Do the workouts as you wrote them in your HZT Planner.

STEP 9. Keep a log of each workout.

STEP 10. Complete monthly self tests.

- Test 1: Sport specific Max HR test
- Test 2: "Improvement effect heart rate" test - hold distance and heart rate constant and measure elapsed time.
- Test 3: Resting HR test
- Test 4: Ambient HR test
- Test 5: Delta HR test

It's time for you to put all of this together into a system with the proper tool for the job - your heart rate monitor. A heart rate monitor is your coach, your personal trainer. It's at your side whenever you wish, giving you the hard data on what your body is experiencing. Your Heart Zone Training success really all depends on you linking it all together - the plan, the workout, the information, the motivation, the results. That's what a heart rate monitor can do for you. It's the link between your mind and your body. It is this dynamic interaction that gives you the power to make it all work and to see the results. It's your personal power tool.

In order to give you the information you need, the heart rate monitor needs to get a little info from you first. So the first thing to do is to set your training zone, the high and low numbers of beats per minute, into the watch portion of your monitor. There are many different models of heart rate monitors, with many different features, so it's difficult to make suggestions as to how you'll set the numbers in any given monitor. Remember, though, that keeping track of your zone numbers is the most basic, essential thing that most heart rate monitors do, so it's always quite simple. And, if in doubt, refer to your owner's manual, even if your manual is hard to read. The low-end heart rate monitors only give you a constant heart rate read-out, so if you use this model you're going to have to memorise your zones and keep the floor and ceiling numbers in your mind.

WORKOUT # 9:

CLIMBING THE INTERVAL LADDER

Introduction. This is one of those really hard workouts, so watch out if you aren't ready to tackle those upper zones. If you're ready to feel the flavour of high performance heart zone training, this workout is a good way to begin your interval training.

Heart zone intervals are similar to the intervals that you may have been doing in the past because they consist of hard and easy timed sessions. The tough part of this workout is that the rest is at the beginning and as you climb up the ladder there is no relief until you hit the top rung.

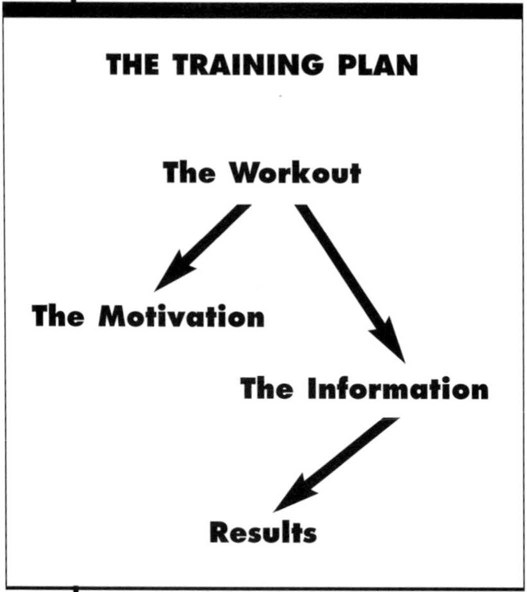

THE TRAINING PLAN

The Workout

The Motivation

The Information

Results

Workout Plan.
This workout is sometimes called a "progression ascent" because you work progressively harder and harder as you ascend to the top of the session. With each step on the ladder, you move up one zone and drop one minute off the interval time. Start out in the warm-up phase by spending five minutes in your Healthy Heart zone (Z1) or 50-60 percent of Max heart rate. After five minutes, move up one zone to the Temperate Zone (Z2) for four minutes. Continue this progression through each zone and end with one minute in your Redline zone (Z5).

If you find this workout is too strenuous, modify it slightly by dropping the Redline zone and shortening each of the other zones by one minute. For those of you who are accustomed to high intensity training, do two or three repeats or repetitions of this workout.

Comment. I personally love the high zones but I'm a lactic acid junkie, so that feeling of complete exhaustion when I finish my redline time is for me the best. Also, I know what the benefits are and that keeps me motivated. By training in the upper zones, I get the performance benefits of improved cardiovascular function and faster speed. I need both of these for competitive performances. However, it really is good for most of us to get a little faster and a little fitter.

The Weight Zone Training Plan

CHAPTER 14

Almost twenty years ago, I read a small, self-published pamphlet titled "Fit or Fat" written by a young man named Covert Bailey. At the time, Covert had just quit his high school teaching job and was looking for a book contract to convert his pamphlet into a real book. Off he went, travelling the roads of America to dunk people in water tanks to measure their percent of body fat, all the while preaching a simple principle: you are either fit or you are fat, and you can't be both.

> Fit or Fat has sold over 4 million copies.

From the time I first read Covert's philosophy, he has been one of my teachers and friends. At one of his televised lectures, he was demonstrating the Fit or Fat "Target Diet," making a series of concentric circles, from the outer circle which was inscribed with the word "suet," or pure animal lard, to an innermost circle with the words "fruits, grains and vegetables." He said on national television that "People like Sally Edwards who exercise dogmatically can eat completely from the outer ring foods. Sally can eat suet all day long." Yeech. Thanks, Covert. You're a good friend and all, but remind me not to take you up on any invitations to eat suet with you.

This was his way of making the point that if you *don't* faithfully exercise aerobically, then you have to eat a specific diet based on the inner, low-fat circles only, with few of the high-fat, outer circle ingredients. I encourage everyone fighting the fat battle to read Bailey's *Target Diet*. It is an excellent approach - eating low-fat foods and high amounts of complex carbohydrates - and the one which we are going to explore here.

WEIGHT ZONE TRAINING TREE

Heart Zone System
Choose this branch if you are ready to
put it all together.

Kaizen Diet
Choose this branch when you are ready
to add a nutrition plan.

Behaviour Plan
Choose this branch when you are ready to
add your habits and behaviours in a new way

Heart Zone Training
Choose this branch if you are ready
to start a fitness program.

Assessment
Start with this branch and learn your
numbers: lean body weight, maximum
heart rate, heart zones, waist to hip ratio

Start
Basal metabolic rate.

If it were possible to melt down the basics of what research and experience have shown to be the most effective, common-sense, long-term weight-loss plan into a single sentence, it would read something like this:

> **Lower the amount of fat you eat and increase the amount of fat you burn exercising.**

That statement is worth posting on your refrigerator. Read it every day.

The nitty gritty here is that there are three things that go hand in hand if you are interested in fat loss - reducing your fat intake to 20%-30% of your total calories; reducing your body fat by exercising especially at 60%-70% Max HR; reducing your total nutrient calories. You see, it's a combination of these basics with a few more factors.

Though not as easy as it might at first appear, you can be successful; but there is one caveat - the time factor. If you think there's an overnight solution to your fat-loss needs, then you are in for yet another dietary disappointment. If you believe that it could take as long to get the fat out and off as it took to get the fat in, then you'll have a chance at success. Practicing Heart Zone Training along with smart eating skills will be the key. The chart below shows you the ratio of fuels burned in each zone.

HZT FAT AND CALORIE BURNING BY ZONES

Percentage of Max HR	Training Zones	Wellness Zones	Zone Numbers	Fuel Burned	RPE	Kcal/ 30 Min
90%-100%	Redline	Performance Zones	Z5	~90% cho / ~10% fat >1% pro	15-20	Can't Sustain
80%-90%	Threshold		Z4	~85% cho / ~15% fat >1% pro	>15	450 kcal
70%-80%	Aerobic	Fitness Zone	Z3	~50% cho / ~50% fat >1% pro	>12	360 kcal
60%-70%	Temperate	Health Zone	Z2	~10% cho / ~85% fat >5% pro	>10	300 kcal
50%-60%	Healthy Heart		Z1	~10% cho / ~85% fat >5% pro	>6	180 kcal

*Approximate for 150 lb. person, walking or running, 20-25% body fat
~means approximately

THE WEIGHT ZONE TRAINING: Skills

One of the foundations of this plan is to learn how to eat "smart" and focus on exercise, not how to diet. In learning to eat, you want to learn how to eat low-fat foods that are high in nutritional value or nutrient dense. First, it's important to pick up some necessary eating and exercising skills, then change your habits.

Saturated Fat

Not liquid at room temperature
Mostly animal sources

beef, butter, cheese, chocolate, cream, custard, fried foods, granola, ice cream, lamb, most meats, milk (whole, 2%,1%), non-dairy creamers, pizza, sauces, sour cream, vegetable and nut oils.

Polyunsaturated Fat

Liquid at room temperature
Fish, nuts, seeds

bagels, breads, corn chips, corn meal, fish, lentils, nuts, popcorn (air pop), potato chips, refried beans, salad dressings, seeds, soybeans, squash, sweet potatoes, tofu, vegetable and nut oils.

Monounsaturated Fat

Liquid at room temperature
Vegetables and nuts

almonds, avocados, bread*, eggs*, lard*, margarine, nuts, oatmeal, pastries*, peanut butter, shortening (vegetable), vegetable and nut oils.
Also high in saturated fat.

You will need to count fat grams, not just calories. Read labels, keeping track of the number of fat grams that you eat until you reach your allocation - your fat gram budget. Eat to feed your lean mass, as many calories as it needs. But - and this is a really, really big "but" - you are limited to a fixed number of fat grams per day, based on the total calories your lean mass requires. If you need to eat 2,000 calories per day, and if 20% of those calories are from fat, then you need to figure out your "fat budget." There are 9 calories of fat per gram, so here's the math:

2,000 calories per day x 20% from fat
= 400 fat calories per day

400 fat calories per day divided by 9 calories per fat gram
= 44 grams of fat per day

That's the 20% fat budget for a 2,000-calorie per day diet - 44 grams. You can use the chart below to find our how many grams of fat you can eat per day, depending on your overall caloric intake. Remember, eat whatever you want, but when you reach your budgeted number of grams of fat for the day, eat no more fat!

Calories Per Day	20% Fat (Grams)	30% Fat (Grams)
1,200	27	40
1,300	29	43
1,400	31	46
1,500	33	50
1,600	36	53
1,700	38	56
1,800	40	60
1,900	42	63
2,000	44	66
2,100	47	70
2,200	49	73
2,300	51	76
2,400	53	80
2,500	56	83
2,600	58	86
2,700	60	90
2,800	62	93
2,900	64	96
3,000	67	100

There's no point in giving you figures below 1,200 calories per day, because it simply isn't healthy to restrict your calories more severely than that (that goes for women; if you're a man, 1,500 calories/day should be your minimum). Circle the number of calories per day you want for your diet plan, and this will determine your daily range of fat grams. For example, if you plan to eat 1,700 calories daily, then your daily fat budget is 38 to 56 grams total.

Generally, the proportion of different dietary fuels should be as follows:

12%-15% Protein
25%-30% Fat
58%-63% Carbohydrates

From 12% to 15% of your calories should come from protein. That means in the example above, in a 2,000 calorie per day diet, 12%, 240 calories or 60 grams, need to be from protein. The remainder of the calories should be from complex carbohydrates - in this example, 63% worth of carbohydrates would be 1,260 calories worth or 315 grams. There is little particular advantage - in health or athletic performance - to further increasing the percentages of carbohydrates or protein or lowering the percentage of dietary fat. Fat is an essential part of our diet and we need a minimum amount for health. According to the Surgeon General's Report on Nutrition and Health, "Adults need a minimum daily intake of 15-25 [fat] grams per day."

Since your goal is to get the excess fat out of your food and to feed and exercise your lean mass, and you know that you have a fixed number of fat grams to eat, this makes the Heart Zone Training diet plan much simpler than many.

Finally, you *have* to start writing it down. That is, you must write down the number of grams of fat you eat, each and every time you eat. You can keep this record in your daily planner or in your exercise log, but you have to keep track. If you want to win your own personal fat battle, learning a few new skills will help. Eventually, when you've changed your eating habits, writing down your fat grams may no longer be necessary, because low-fat eating will have become integrated into your lifestyle.

You also can learn better eating by reading books to support the plan. Definitely use a low-fat cookbook to provide you with new and different menus. You'll also need a fat gram-counter so you can keep track of how much fat is in different foods.

J. Bellerson's The Complete and Up-To-Date Fat Book lets you keep track of the grams of fat in over 25,000 foods.

THE WEIGHT ZONE TRAINING: Habits

The second part of the Weight Zone Training weight-management plan depends on your developing some new habits.

Look for foods that are marked with the words "low fat" or "no fat." It's easier to find low-fat choices for all sorts of prepared foods that meet the government's low- or no-fat criteria. Make your snack choices conscious ones, such as air-popped popcorn with seasonings, no-oil tortilla chips, low-fat pretzels, or fat-free popsicles or cookies.

Another good habit is reading labels. In addition to letting you know how much fat you are getting from a particular food, nutritional labels also can help you select the type of fats: good fats or bad. There are three types of fat - monounsaturated, polyunsaturated and saturated - and you want to become fast friends with the unsaturated ones. Unsaturated fats are those that are liquid at room temperature.

There are two kinds of fatty acids that our bodies use: non-essential (we make these) and essential fatty acids (we get these from our foods). Essential fatty acids are unsaturated and necessary for proper bodily functions such as manufacturing antibodies, carrying fat-soluble vitamins, protecting organs, digestion, and more. We can get all of the fatty acids we need from unsaturated fat - we don't need one single gram of saturated fat in our diets.

Staying away from hydrogenated fat is another good habit to get into. Hydrogenation is a process whereby good, unsaturated fat is made into unacceptable, saturated fat. Avoid it. Read the labels and select the unsaturated fat - but remember, *any* gram of fat, good or bad, contains 9 calories per gram, regardless of its type. All calories from whatever source count in the weight balancing equation.

When you read labels, make it a habit to look at the heading "% Daily Value" and to choose foods that are 5% or less in the "Total Fat" category. That way, if you

for your information:

Fat is an efficient food - too efficient. It takes less than 5% of its own calories to digest, while carbohydrates require about 25% of their calories to be metabolised.

were to eat one serving of 20 different foods per day, each totalling 5% or less of your total fat intake, you still wouldn't go over 100% of your budgeted fat calories. For some, noting fat percentages when they shop is easier than counting fat grams.

Get into the habit of asking questions when you buy food. For example, at our local bagel bakery, there may be a notebook available giving a complete nutritional breakdown for each type of bagel. My favourite cinnamon and raisin bagel has 360 calories and 1 gram of fat while my second-favourite, sesame seed bagel has 330 calories and 1.8 grams of fat.

Make it a habit to carry food with you that fit your diet plan. Pack yourself a food bag when you leave the house - those mesh grocery bags work well. Load it up with five pieces of fruit, plenty of low-fat cookies and crackers, some carrots, and a source of a moderate amount of protein-rich foods (such as low-fat cheese sticks or yogurt) and you'll never be hungry. Trouble lurks when you get hungry and don't have low fat and lower calorie food easily available. If you have your trusty food bag with you, you can head off dietary trouble before it sends you off course.

Z2 TEMPERATE ZONE: Getting the Fat Out

Okay, next step. You've got the food down, so now it's time to begin the Fat Burning exercise plan. The fat burning zones are your three lowest ones: Z1-Z3. The Temperate zone is 60%-70% of your Max HR, remember. You can hang out there easily with almost any activity you enjoy: cycling, walking, swimming, skating, skiing, snowshoeing, hiking, housework (okay, maybe you don't enjoy this one), circuit weight training, exercise machines, aerobic gardening, and working out with video fitness programs.

Z1 through Z3 are your best fat burning zones. To begin with, you want to stay in these cool and moderate zones for at least 10-20 minutes a day.

The body adapts to whatever stimulus you introduce it to - with each day, your new program will become easier. As your body adapts to 10-20 minutes per day, which usually takes 2–4 weeks of regular exercise, you will notice how quickly the time goes by and that you're eager to stay longer in the fat burning zones. For weight loss purposes, the key is to extend the length of time that you are in the zones, *not* to go into the higher zones.

For fat to be freed from its fat cells, it needs low-intensity exercise for progressively longer and longer periods of time. When 20 minutes seems too short, move on to the next phase of your training. Extend the length of time that you are training. If you can extend your workout to 30 minutes a day, simply adding ten minutes to your workout times, you'll be burning half again as many fat calories as before. You'll also be giving your fat cells more time to release fat molecules and your bloodstream more time to carry them to your muscles where they will be readily metabolised.

Your goal is to extend your exercise time - maybe to 40 minutes a day all at one time or in two different workout periods. It doesn't really matter if it is twice a day for 20 minutes or any variation thereof. What matters is "time in zone" - that you are hanging out in the fat burning zones (Z1-Z3) for as long as possible. If you become a real aficionado of Heart Zone Training, hang out as long as you want in the fat burning zones - it will only do you more and more good. But at first, just begin your program with 10-20 minutes. You'll find that by doing so you will get immediate success and be rewarded by various benefits from the health continuum: lower blood pressure, lower resting heart rate, lower percentage of body fat, stabilised body weight, and lower (LDL or "bad") cholesterol.

EMOTIONS IN MOTION

There is a third component to weight loss that we need to address briefly, even though it deserves much more attention than we can provide for here. Weight loss or fat loss is an emotional as much as a physical issue. There may be major self-image issues for you to resolve. Thankfully, this is one of the great aspects of Heart Zone Training. It will make you feel better about yourself emotionally, which further reinforces your confidence to stay with it.

MY STORY,
by Lisa Allen

Psychologists say that gaining weight after marriage and motherhood is no accident. There are many complex, tangled emotional issues involved. For me, understanding intellectually what made my weight gain happen did not give me the tools to make it go away or stop continuing.

I had amassed 75 extra pounds over the five years since my marriage and the birth of my two children. I tried the counting calories approach - dieting caused more problems than it ever solved. I'd lose a fast five, hang in there and starve until ten came off. But then the inevitable loss of willpower would come and bingo, I'd put on fifteen. If my math is right, that would be a net gain of five, with a bonus of a slowed metabolism that would hang onto everything I ate for fear of being starved again.

I actually did lose something - my self esteem. The scenario is quite familiar to anyone who has ever tried to lose weight. I felt alone, frightened, and downright miserable. How could I have gone from being a fit National Champion in down river marathon canoeing, a marathon runner, and an athlete extraordinaire to being 75 pounds overweight? I would look in the mirror and see a woman I didn't recognise staring back at me.

I knew that I had to exercise, and I tried. The problem was that I had this concept that exercise was something you did as fast as you could for as long as you could, and anything less was not worth doing. I would start running or doing aerobics and go like a maniac until I would aggravate a previous back injury. Forced to lay off exercise for weeks at a time, I felt my weight was taking control of my body and my life.

The day my husband came home with a heart rate monitor and a companion book by Sally changed my life forever. I read the book and discovered that to lose weight I didn't need to go at break-neck speed. Exercising in the Fat Burning zone allowed me to go slowly enough that I could endure longer periods of exercise and easy enough not to reinjure my back. I didn't even get up into the Aerobic zone for the first six months.

At about the same time, I began to read about low-fat eating regimens. I learned to eat rather than diet. The combination of low-fat eating and heart-rate monitored exercise was like working both sides of an equation and coming up with exactly the right answer: the weight started melting off.

I went slowly, but steadily. It took me 18 months to lose all the weight, but today I remain 135 pounds with only 16% body fat. I demonstrated that aphorism that sometimes "slow and steady wins the race." I have made peace with food, and aside from monitoring my fat intake, I rarely give it a second thought. I eat as much low-fat or non-fat food as I want when I'm hungry, and there is not one iota of guilt. Heart-rate monitored exercise has been the true key to my continued success.

Rewards are important, and when you deserve one, take it. That applies to more than just this program, but to the bigger picture as well. The greatest reward for me is when someone writes me or comes into my life like Lisa with her success story of getting the fat out of her diet and her body. But, every once in a while there is a reward that is even more cherished than this one. And this is when the Lisas of the world share their experiences with others so that they can experience the same successes that they did.

Weight management success by using a heart rate monitor, hanging out in the fat burning zones Z1-Z3 for a year and a half, and living a fat gram-counting life, has been a sweet victory for Lisa. But even better, she's sharing that experience with others. Lisa has completed her certificate to teach exercise and be a personal trainer, and she has been working since her successful experience with those who can relate to going from 220 pounds to her ideal body weight of 135 pounds and eating enough to satisfy her healthy appetite. She is living proof of the low-fat high-fit lifestyle.

Whether the Weight Zone Training plan results in a change in your life's work or merely a change in your clothes size, it *will* change both you and your lifestyle. When we change, all things change.

Workout # 10:
For Beginners.

Introduction. A lot of us simply don't have the time to train but we want to stay fit and race at high levels of performance. If you fit this description, interval training or high intensity exercise should be the cornerstone of your training plan. But you have to work up to this level and not just jump in.

In the beginning, your goal should be one heart rate interval workout a week. Later, you can add more time in the top two zones: Threshold (80-90 percent of Max HR) and Redline (90-100 percent of Max HR).

To do the following interval workouts effectively you must know your sports specific Max HR and calculate each of your training zones. Keep this information for future reference in your training log or computer data base. Here are interval workouts for the three sports of triathlon.

SWIMMING

Warm up with a steady state swim for five minutes at 60-70 percent of Max HR. Start interval session with six to eight, 50-yard repeats coming in on 90 percent of Max HR. Rest after each repeat until your HR recovers to 80 percent then push off for the next repeat.

Next, do four 100-yard repeats and drop the intensity by 5 percent. That is, finish your swim repeats at 85 percent of Max HR and start the next one at 75 percent.

Finish the set with one 500-yard steady state swim at 80 percent of Max HR. Cool down the same as the warm-up.

CYCLING

Warm up for ten minutes at 50-60 percent of your Max HR. Pick up the cadence and load to 85 percent of Max HR and hold for four minutes then drop back to 70 percent of Max HR for four minutes. Do this 8-minute repeat two to four times. Warm down by spinning at 60 percent of Max HR until you are home.

RUNNING

Warm up at 50-60 percent of Max HR for at least 10 minutes. Next, increase the intensity up to 90 percent of Max HR and hold for one minute before easing down to 60 percent of Max HR for two minutes. Repeat this four times and then warm down at 50 percent of Max HR. As this session becomes easier, add time to the work interval and keep the rest time as you transfer between a 1:2 to 2:1 to 2:2 ratio of work to rest.

Comment. Don't get too carried away initially with your interval training. On the good side, it gets you in great shape, fast. On the negative side, too much leads to overtraining and a decrease in fitness. Stay on the good side of heart zone training by training up the training tree.

For Competitive Athletes

If you exercise regularly, you are an athlete. Believe it, take pride in it, because you are.

That being said, we should note that there are different types of athletes: competitive and non-competitive ones. Training for high performance is mainly the domain of competitive athletes, whether they are competing against other athletes, the time clock, or themselves. If you are currently a competitive athlete, by all means, jump into this chapter and go! If you are a non-competitive, health or fitness athlete, you don't *need* to read this chapter, but we do recommend skimming it for the tidbits which will come in handy - if not now, then down the line.

INTERVALS

The first tool in a high performance program is intervals. Intervals add variety both in your training and in your training benefits (adaptations) so you can most efficiently improve your fitness level. If you are not doing interval training as part of your schedule now, it's time to start.

"Interval" can be a somewhat muddled term. By definition, interval training is a type of workout which consists of a period of high intensity exercise followed by a period of rest - complete or incomplete rest. Several intervals are called a *repetition* (reps). Several repetitions are called a *set*. Following each exercise interval is a *recovery time* (rest) which allows for recuperations.

Intervals are written in a standard way called coaches shorthand.

Seems confusing at first. Go to your master's swim workout and you'll see this coaches shorthand posted on a workout board.

One of the best ways to understand intervals is to diagram it as follows:

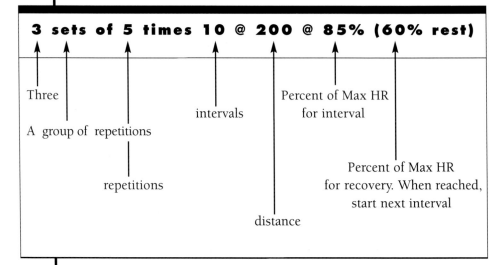

3 sets of 5 times 10 @ 200 @ 85% (60% rest)

Three

A group of repetitions

intervals

Percent of Max HR for interval

repetitions

Percent of Max HR for recovery. When reached, start next interval

distance

The interval training system has been supported by a tremendous amount of research to validate the premise that by raising and lowering your heart rate or workloads during a single workout, multiple zone benefits occur. Among the most basic of these benefits are:

- Increased endurance ability or aerobic capacity, which is measured by the amount of oxygen that you can use (VO_2max).
- Increased total number of calories burned if you increase your intensity.
- Increased fun, because you add variety to your workout.
- Increased focus on your training because of the need to watch for time and intensity variations, which seems to make the time go by faster.

But, there is even more benefit to you depending on the type of interval training that you might do.

There are four different types of intervals, defined by their duration: short or sprint intervals, middle-distance intervals, long intervals, and endurance intervals. The four different interval types each affect different energy systems. Energy systems are the means by which the body transports and converts various fuels into energy. That's the primary point of doing intervals: to train the energy systems to utilise specific fuels and deliver nutrients to your muscles more efficiently. You are actually training your fuel system as much if not more than the specific muscles.

To understand the different types of intervals, here's a more complete explanation.

Sprint and Middle-Distance Intervals benefits:
- Increased anaerobic enzyme activity
- Increased lactate tolerance (pH levels)
- Increased specific muscle strength in the specific muscles used
- Increased power of fast-twitch muscle fibres (Type II)
- Increased phosphagen utilisation   (ATP-PC)

Long and Endurance Intervals benefits:
- Increased anaerobic threshold heart rate
- Increased amount of time spent at higher percentages of VO_2max
- Increased lactate threshold and tolerance
- Increased number of mitochondria (density of mitochondria)
- Increased oxygen transport to and through the membranes
- Increased amount of oxidative enzyme activity
- Increased glycogen sparing ability

The table on the following page further explains the differences between each type of interval.

There are four more important pieces to high performance interval-based training: 1) how many reps or total number of intervals, 2) how much time for rest between intervals, 3) the type of rest in-between reps, and 4) the work-to-rest ratio in each interval. When you have these pieces you can create a variety of interval workouts to match your goals. The table on the next page illustrates the typical characteristics of the respective types of intervals.

ZONES AND INTERVALS

Type of Interval	Heart Zone	Energy Systems Affected	Time in Zone (TIZ)	Name of Interval
Short	Max HR Number	ATP-PC (phosphagen)	<10 seconds	Wind Sprints
Middle	Upper Z5 Redline	Glycolysis (lactic acid)	10 sec–1 minute	Red Line Intervals
Long	Lower Z5 Redline	Mitochondrial (function)	1–5 minutes	Strength intervals
Endurance	Z3-Z5	Oxidative (enzymes)	5–15 minutes	Cardio intervals

There are two types of rest: complete and active. After the interval is over, you take a break or rest interval to allow time for your heart rate to drop to a lower zone. This is called a "recovery period" or recovery interval, and it allows your body to recover from the intensity of the interval, to shuttle away some lactic acid, and to resupply the muscles with fuel. Complete rest means that you slow to a near stop, while active rest means that you slow down but you continue to move - that would be a walk or jog if you were running. Active rest for a cyclist means to shift down to lower gears and spin easy. Active rest to a swimmer means to continue to swim but using a different stroke for recovery.

Here's an example. Let's say you want to do a long interval workout day. You are a swimmer and usually you like to swim continuously for the amount of time you have - say 20 minutes. You're ready for a change and want to exercise a different energy system with high performance heart zone intervals. Today you want to take that same amount of time, 20 minutes, but this time you are going to break it into five different parts. Your first five

Type of Interval	# of reps	Number of Sets	How Much Rest	Type of Rest	Work-to Rest Ratio
Short	4-5	20–25	5 sec–1.5 min	Complete	1 : 3
Middle	3-4	8–10+	20 sec–2 min	Active	1 : 2
Long	2-5	6–10+	1 min–5 min	Active	1 : 1
Endurance	1-2	2–6+	2 min–10 min	Active	2 : 1

minutes is a warm-up of mixed strokes. You then start two sets of five-minute intervals by increasing the intensity of your pace by about 5-10 beats per minute, with a 3-minute active rest during the break between the two intervals. After completing the second of the two high-intensity intervals you take your warm-down swim. If we were to diagram that workout it would be as shown on chart:

You might ask what additional benefit you gain for the tradeoff in complexity with long interval training. The great news is that you are getting new benefits with each of the heart rate zones you're now exercising in. The new zones challenge different energy systems and, sure enough, the body responds to your new regimen with adaptation – the specific energy system or muscle fibres involved change and improve their fuel utilisation, becoming stronger, fitter, and more efficient to meet the work-load imposed upon them. In other words, they can train at higher workloads and perform better, and *you* can race faster.

Looking at each of the four different intervals respectively, here's what you are trying to accomplish:

• **Endurance Intervals.** These are the very long repeat work-outs at lower percentages of your Max HR. A good example would be cross-country ski intervals – loop format. If your loop is 1–2 km, then your cardio interval might be 5 sets of these at 80%-85% of Max

CONTINUOUS INTERVAL		VS.		LONG INTERVAL	
1 set x 20 minutes	Intervals	Activity	Time	Heart Rate	Heart Zone
HR = 70% Max HR	1	Warm Up	5 min	50%-70% Max HR	Z1-Z3
	1	Swim	5 min	85% Max HR	Z4
	1	Active Rest	3 min	60% Max HR	Z2
	1	Swim	5 min	85% Max HR	Z4
	1	Warm Down	2 min	60% Max HR	Z2
	5 intervals			20 min.	

HR with a 3-minute active rest recovery between loops. This workout simulates racing conditions and results in improvement in your oxygen uptake. If you are a marathoner, this is key interval workout for you if you want to improve your time. The table below schematically illustrates endurance intervals.

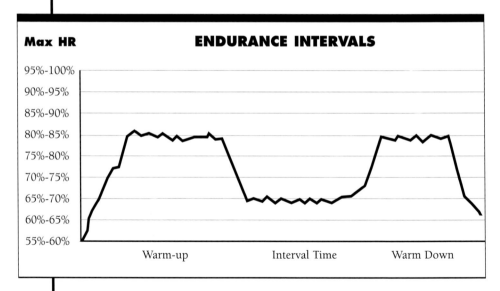

•Long Intervals. These are less lengthy intervals at slightly faster than your race pace or at heart rates about 5 bpm above your long race heart rates. The purpose is to challenge your mitochondria to continue to produce energy at very high rates of demand. Typically, the effort interval is between a minute and five minutes and the rest interval is equal to it. Because the intensity of the interval is slightly above your anaerobic threshold heart rate, you are working in an oxygen debt condition and must allow enough rest to repay this oxygen loan. If you are a 10K athlete, this will probably be your most important interval session. The table below demonstrates interval training sessions.

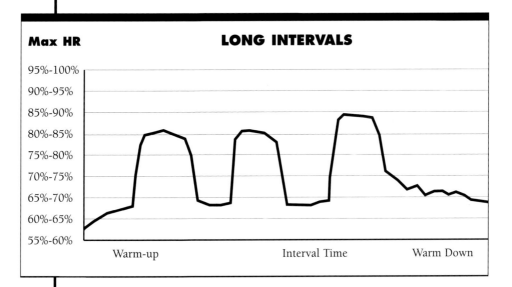

• **Middle Intervals.** These are the intervals for the middle-distance sprint athletes like the 100-meter swimmers and the 400-meter runners. The reason that these intervals are specific to these athletes is that they have the greatest need to improve their anaerobic glycolytic energy system - their ability to tolerate high levels of lactic acid. To develop this ability, middle intervals are a must. Middle distance athletes' training must be event specific, and their intervals can last from 10 seconds to one minute, with the recovery interval twice the length of the effort interval. This is a fast interval and you might well see your Max HR on your heart rate monitor in the last few seconds. Because heart rate monitors work by averaging heart rates every 3-5 seconds depending on the model, your heart rate is actually faster than the monitor reads because of the lag time involved. The active recovery period is important. Continuing to move during the recovery helps with the removal of the lactic acid from the muscle tissues. This lactic acid is transported from the working muscles to the liver and other organs. At the liver, it is resynthesized into glucose, which reenters the blood stream and is transported back to the working muscles for fuel. This is called the "Cori cycle" and provides a benefit to middle-distance athletes who rely primarily on glucose for their energy. The following table shows you the pattern of a middle interval.

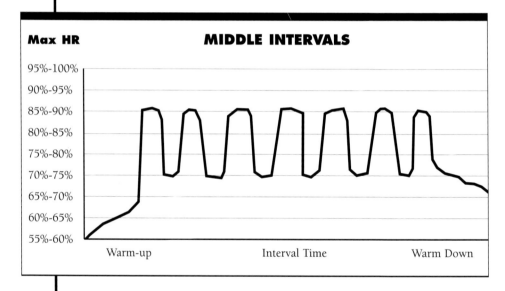

•**Short Intervals.** For sprint-distance athletes, the primary adaptation that needs to occur is to enhance their bodies' abilities to provide immediate bursts of quick energy derived from the creatine phosphate (CP) system (anaerobic phosphagen). You only have enough CP stored for about 10 seconds of high-intensity exercise. Therefore, for these interval sets, all the effort intervals need to be no more than 10 seconds in length with about three times that amount of time for recovery. Recovery needs to be complete rest, with little to no movement, to allow for the resynthesis of intramuscular phosphates (such as ATP and creatine phosphate). This system recovers quickly when you stop, typically requiring about 30 seconds. These are all out sprint intervals - throw your heart rate monitor to the winds. In a 10-second interval you are totally driving sport-specific muscles and not your heart. However, remember that your heart is a "work now/pay now" muscle, so it is probably reaching close to maximum even though your heart rate monitor may not be presenting the data this way. Your goal is to build up to 20-25 repeats of this interval. It is extremely taxing and *not* for those just starting to learn interval training.

For the newly-converted interval trainers, start with the long or endurance intervals. They are more enjoyable and cover much lower heart rate numbers. You might even begin with a "fartlek," because they are as much for fun as for changing heart rate intensity. "Fartlek" is a Scandinavian term for "speed play," and it is just that: it playfully increases and decreases your heart's and your body's speed to obtain some of the benefits of intervals but with more fun attached. A good example of a fartlek workout is the telephone pole fartlek. After you warm up, do a 10-20 bpm pick-up to the next pole and then slow back down to the following pole for recovery and repeat. If you don't have telephone poles, then use mailboxes, fence posts, or sign posts.

As you get more accustomed to intervals, try the shorter ones and feel the differences. Each of the four intervals taxes a different energy system. Remember that, and you'll feel the experience accordingly.

Intervals can be helpful for almost all individuals who are training. For those who are part of a special population such as the physically challenged or rehabilitation patients, interval exercise can help raise your aerobic fitness levels without the stress on your systems of continued mid- or high-range heart rates. The latest research shows that several, shorter intervals can result in some of the same adaptations as fewer, longer intervals. You don't even have to do them back-to-back. It's been repeatedly shown that five minutes a day, three to six times a day is just about as good a workout as one session of 15-30 minutes.

If a single workout or a string of them is missed, don't go back and try to make any of them up. If you miss some, and we all do, it's okay. You may need to rework your training schedule because, if it doesn't fit your time and your lifestyle schedule, it won't work for you. Busy people all struggle to juggle their limited time, but it can fit if you will make it fit. You can wake early and work out during eating periods and eat during working periods; you can even have a personal life by inviting your partner to train with you. It's that simple - make your training tree a part of your lifestyle.

Periodisation: Periodisation is a method of training in which the volume (frequency times time) of training and the relative percentage of each training hour spent in various zones changes in relation to both the short term and long term goals of the individual. For example, a 21-day periodisation for a running plan might look like this:

Training Days	Weekly Exercise Volume (Running)
7 days	50 miles
7 days	70 miles
7 days	30 miles
21 total days	Average: 50 miles/week

In fact, HZT Point System easily allows for periodisation in training by weekly changing points earned such as weeks that cycle 500 points, 1,000 points, 1,500 points.

The Guideline Rules of High-Performance Heart Zone Training

As you progress through the Heart Zone Training system, there are a few standards or rules that need to be heeded. Following these guidelines will make an especially big difference as you climb onto the peaking and racing branches of your training.

RULE 1. 24-Hour Rule. If you are cross-training, you can do a Z5 or upper Z4 workout every 24 hours if it involves a different activity.

RULE 2. 48-Hour Rule. After a Redline or upper Z4 workout, you need to take a 48-hour break before you can train again in this specific activity. The reason is that the specific muscle recovery process requires 48 hours for replenishment.

Rules and Guidelines.

These rules are meant to be your guide and not the law – staying within them is safe but they are only guidelines.

RULE 3. 10% Rule. A single day's Redline workout should not exceed 10% of the total zone time for the week.

RULE 4. 50% Rule. The total Z4 and Z5 workout time should not exceed 25%-50% of your total training time.

RULE 5. Rate Not Pace. It's more important to know your heart rate than your velocity or pace. That is, it is better to know at what percentage of your maximum heart rate you are training than your speed.

RULE 6. At-About-Around. If the goal (and the true definition of cardiovascular fitness) is to raise your anaerobic threshold heart rate as close as possible to your maximum heart rate, then high performance trainers who have reached the speed branch on the training tree need to spend at least 25% of their weekly time at-about-around their anaerobic threshold heart rate. Remember, this is a moving heart rate number; as you get fitter it moves toward your maximum heart rate, and one of the best ways to raise your anaerobic threshold is to train as close as possible to it.

RULE 7. Heart Sparing. Your upper heart rate limits are very stressful on *every* system in your body - over-training is frequently the result of spending too much time in the upper two zones. It's with a blend of the upper and lower zones and by consciously calculating how much time you train in the upper zones that you practice good heart-sparing training.

RULE 8. Zones Are Progressive. Heart zones are positive and progressive stressors to the training system. As a result, the body learns to adapt to these stresses and improve. The three systems stressed are muscles, energy, and cardiovascular. By progressively increasing the intensity component, improvement occurs sequentially.

RULE 9. Narrow Your Zones. The narrower you can shrink the zones, the more precise your training. Ultimately, the goal is to establish specific individual heart rates which are key training indexes to use in ultra high performance training. If you narrow the Threshold zone from a big 20-beat window down to a narrow five-beat window that includes the anaerobic threshold point, then train at-about-around that point, you have learned fine-tuned training.

RULE 10. The 5-Beat Rule. If your morning resting heart rate (before you get out of bed) is 5 beats above your normal average, drop your training for the day by at least one zone or take a complete rest day. An incremental increased resting heart rate is an excellent indicator of over-stressing your body's systems and is a warning sign or a wake-up signal to back off.

RULE 11. Highest Sustainable Heart Rate. One of the secrets of heart rate racing is to maintain the highest heart rate number that you can sustain over the entire time period of the event. Your highest sustainable heart rate is an individual heart rate number; for high-performance athletes, it's a number you pick out of your imagination or your dreams or aspiration, but in reality it is a heart rate number that you have trained at and know intimately because it is that borderline heart rate that could take you to either side: success or blowup. *Train and know well your highest sustainable heart rate before the race.* Time trial this heart rate number. For races longer than 20 minutes in duration, it is probably below your AT HR depending on environmental factors.

RULE 12. As training intensity increases, training volume decreases. Training intensity identifies the quality of exercise effort and is related inversely to volume. If you are training more time in the higher zones then you need to decrease the quantity of training done during the specific workout session (training volume).

IT'S THE LINK

The only real way to know if high-performance Heart Zone Training works is to follow it and then take it to the starting line with you. That's what I did when I set my goal to win the master's division of the 1991 Ironman Triathlon. After enough maximum sustainable heart rate time trials to make you disgusted, I set my racing heart rates within very, very narrow windows: 150-155 bpm on the bike (for a 6-hour period) and at 172 bpm on the 26.2-mile run (covering about 3.5 hours).

In this ultra-distance triathlon in Hawaii, there are two factors to beware of: cumulative fatigue and environmental extremes (extreme heat with high humidity). I factored both of these conditions into my decision and set my maximum sustainable heart rates accordingly. The race then became one between me and my heart rate monitor - not the competition.

As I rode my bike on the out-and-back race course, I was passed by hundreds of cyclists (there were 1,500 athletes in the race). I didn't allow that to affect my plan, although it always takes its toll emotionally. Rather, I stared at my friend the monitor for the entire ride, always keeping my heart rate within the narrow window of 150-155 bpm. On the uphills, I had to go extremely slow; on the downhills I had to work hard to stay within my heart zone window. On the return leg of the bike course, I passed the hundreds of cyclists who'd previously whipped by me as I steadily followed my heart rate and avoided the debilitation of extreme fatigue from racing in a zone higher than I could sustain.

I started the run and locked into my 172 bpm racing heart

rate. It was comfortable, but my legs were tired. Someone from the crowd yelled out that I was in fifth place and that the lead woman had 27 minutes on me. Calculating the 26 miles in a marathon, I figured that I would have to outrun her by a minute a mile - that would be difficult since I had raced her before and her primary event was marathons. I got depressed. I looked down at my monitor and, though I felt like I was exerting myself as much as before, my emotions took their toll. It read only 153 bpm.

What are you supposed to do in this situation? When you are racing and you go into a down period during the race and start to lose hope - what do you do? The answer is always the same. Reach down to that place deep inside yourself and find the internal power and strength to go back to your race plan. I worked out the effect of the news of fifth place and 27 minutes and went back to 172 bpm. I believed at that point that my race plan would work.

At the halfway point, someone shouted out that I was in second place and she had a 15-minute lead. When you are physically tired, it's very difficult to calculate numbers but this math was simple - I was catching her but not fast enough to cross the finish line ahead of her. I looked down at my wrist and the monitor that should have been locked in at 172 bpm now read 145 bpm. Depression was getting my heart rate down again. I had slowed my pace.

At this point, all high-performance athletes know exactly what to do. You can either toss your race plan to the wind and go for it, or you stick to it. Those who win always stick to the game plan. But cumulative fatigue was setting in as fast as the heat and the hours of high heart rate and doubt. This was a race of the mind as much as of the heart.

At mile 22 on the marathon course, I spotted her. Within minutes I was by her side, and I said hello as I ran beyond. As I pulled ahead, I didn't look back, but I did look down at my heart rate reading - 185 bpm, or 96% of my Max HR (in running). That's dangerous ground, but that's what happens when you're so excited by the moment and so exhausted from 10-plus hours of racing.

This created a new problem in the race plan. What do you do when your heart rate is 185 bpm and you're leading? At this point, all high-performance athletes do the exact same thing. It's at this moment when you are running mere moments away from victory that you toss your monitor to the wind and you run on *heart,* not on rate.

I crossed the finish line and won the race by 90 seconds, after 11 hours of racing, because I had a heart rate monitor and she didn't.

Workout # 11:
SIZZLING HOT WORKOUT

Introduction. This is a workout for those of you who want to get faster...a lot faster. As we have mentioned previously, to get faster you need to follow the "at-about-around" principle by training at-about-or-around your anaerobic threshold heart rate (AT HR). You can get faster by spending more of your training time above your AT HR than at or about it.

Workout Plan. This 30-minute interval workout is called "Sizzling Hot" because it's almost all in your Redline Zone (90-100 percent of Max HR) and 20 minutes are spent above your AT HR. The Redline Zone is a very high intensity zone so you can't stay there long and a rest period is needed after each interval.

You need to be training on a regular program before you attempt any sizzling hot interval workouts. The workout is commonly called a "ladder" but rather than being based on time or distance, it uses HR.

To do this workout you will need to know your AT HR. The following field test will give you a ballpark estimate. This test, which consists of two times 20 minutes at the fastest you can go, must be completed on the same workout session.

Set your monitor so it will give you an average of each 20 minute test. After warming up, run your first 20 minute test then note the average HR. Take a jog rest for at least five minutes then do another 20 minutes as fast as you can go. The average HR of the second test should be within five beats of the first test. Your ballpark AT HR estimate is the average of your two field tests. Now that you know your AT HR, here's the sizzling workout as shown in the chart.

WORKOUT

Interval	Intensity	Exercise Time	Rest Time
#1	AT HR + 2 bpm	8 minutes	2 minutes
#2	AT HR + 4 bpm	6 minutes	3 minutes
#3	AT HR + 6 bpm	4 minutes	3 minutes
#4	AT HR + 8 bpm	2 minutes	2 minutes

Comment. It is important to look at the work to rest ratio when doing high intensity, long intervals. Overall, this workout consists of 2:1 work to rest ratio. As the workload (intensity) increases, the work interval (exercise time) decreases.

Again, this is a workout where you are putting the pedal to the floor at near full forward speed.

Be careful, it will get you fitter and faster, but it's also a workout which requires a day of rest for recovery. Pay attention to your resting HR the next day to make sure you haven't over-stressed the system.

Sex and
The Heart Zones

Why would anyone want to find out what their heart rates are during sex? What's more, why would anyone want to talk about it?

Sex may be a touchy subject (pun intended!), but for some people it's a serious one. The topic comes up routinely for cardiac rehabilitation patients - any perceived marked elevation of heart rate for these folks can be a cause for fear and anxiety, and you can just imagine how that contributes to their sexual experience and peace of mind.

For others of us, the sex-heart rate relationship may not be as weighty a topic, but we still find it pretty interesting (I, for one, am tired of the fact that researchers seem to know more about the sexual habits of baboons than of humans). And for many competitive athletes, who wear their heart rate monitors continuously, observing the effects of sex on their heart rates is something they couldn't help but notice.

When it comes down to the facts on the matter, however, the surprising thing is how far apart perception and reality are. Exercise isn't the only topic obscured by our paradigms, after all!

Several months ago, at the invitation of my friend Lyle, a four-time Olympic biathlete, we took off for a Threshold zone workout running the hills in Portland, Oregon. On one particularly gnarly uphill I jumped on the topic, asking if, as a man, he had a mental perception as to what his heart rate was at the time of climax. Not a question one might ask of strangers, true, but Lyle isn't.

He responded that almost all of his cross-country skiing friends use heart rate monitors, some of them regularly sleeping with their chest straps and wrist monitors on, and that sex and heart rate zones is occasionally a topic of their discussion. Lyle said it is common for the men to express a certain frustration and astonishment at the low heart rate numbers their monitors record during sex. (Remember, these are competitive athletes; they like and are accustomed to seeing high numbers on their heart rate monitors. Lyle describes this as the "competitive heart rates" phenomenon, a common theme among competitive individuals.) Lyle is quick to add that there appears to be no correlation, and, if anything, a reverse correlation between high heart rates during sex and sexual performance. After all says Lyle, "the heart rate does go high on a long, slow distance workout."

If you're bold, you too, could try asking a close friend who is comfortable with the topic to just guess at the average heart rate for men and women during intercourse. I've found that the result is always the same: the men predict very high heart rate numbers, and the women chuckle and chide them, usually predicting low numbers.

The fact is, we know more about the effects of exercise on athletes and astronauts than we do about the effect of *sexual* exercise on people in their bedrooms. There is even less information available about sexual activity in people who have experienced heart disease. That's because it's not easy to study humans and sexual activity without running into all kinds of obstacles – psychological, physiological, and ethical. From the published research studies, the average heart rate for men in the "on top" position is 117 beats per minute for about 10-20 seconds of orgasm.

Now, you probably want to know why it's so low.

The reason that average heart rates are so low is probably as much a matter of position and the muscles involved as individuals' perception of energy expenditure or the amount of perspiration released. During sexual activity, people are usually in a horizontal position, and they are not using the large muscle groups that are involved in cross-country skiing, swimming, or walking. They are also usually not, in metabolic terms, in a "steady state" of exertion, especially during the very brief, peak heart-rate period of orgasm.

FACTS AND FIGURES

Before quoting additional research, there are a few other facts that should be noted. First, it's always difficult to quantify sexual activity because of the emotional factors that can distort the physiological reactions and a cause a high degree of variation. Second, there is much less research data about the sex-heart rate connection in women than in men, because while the male sexual response is readily apparent, the female response isn't. Third, it is known that age plays a role in sexual response as well, but perhaps due to the small scale of most sex-heart rate studies, age data is not always taken into account. Fourth, there are *many* other factors that can affect the rate of sexual response, including depression (which is more common among those with heart disease), prescription or illicit drug use, or alcohol use. Keep in mind, too, the variability among people's resting heart rates - which can be as low as 30 beats per minute in the extremely fit and over 100 beats per minute in the sedentary low fit-and their maximum heart rates; this same variability will hold true for their average heart rates at the peak of sexual stimulation.

The last facts you should keep in mind are that the physiological response to sexual activity can be divided into four phases: (1) arousal/foreplay, (2) plateau, (3) orgasm, and (4) resolution. In the healthy population, the response to sexual intercourse is an increase in heart rate, blood pressure and respiratory rate. In general, this increase is gradual during arousal, increases rapidly in the minute preceding orgasm, peaks briefly during orgasm, and then rapidly declines to resting level within two or three minutes.

• In 1966, Masters and Johnson reported heart rates at orgasm in a range of 110-189 bpm. However, they didn't state the average values, how many people were measured, the age of the subjects, or any other variables.

• Hellerstein and Friedman, in 1970, using a portable electrocardiogram (ECG), reported a mean peak heart rate at orgasm of 117 bpm (range of 90-144 bpm). They recorded an average heart rate of 87 bpm two minutes before, 110 bpm one minute before, 97 bpm one minute after, and 85 bpm two minutes after orgasm. These researchers also measured VO$_2$ levels of their subjects to measure energy expenditure during sexual activity. They found that the highest oxygen intakes were 16 ml/kg/min. and the two-minutes-before and two-minutes-after values were 12 ml/kg/min. This energy expenditure is the same as walking a 15-minute per mile pace on flat terrain and for all but the most exceptional men - may amount to the equivalent energy expended in walking only several blocks at this pace.

• Jackson, using a ECG on the same 14 patients before and after taking beta-blockers (medication that prevents high heart rates), noted the average peak heart rate was 124 bpm before and 122 bpm after the medication was administered.

• Nemec used a portable ECG recorder and automatic ultra-sonic recorder to study the heart rate and blood pressure responses of 10 men (ages 24-40 years) during four episodes of sexual intercourse with their wives. Two sessions were with the man on top and two sessions were with the man on bottom. Both positions were tested because physicians commonly counsel their cardiac rehabilitation patients to assume a more passive (on bottom) position to avoid overexertion. There was no significant difference between the two positions. The average heart rates for the men were 117 bpm man-on-top, and 114 bpm in the man-on-bottom position. These findings are illustrated in the figure on the following page.

• Stein took a group of 16 men aged 46-54 years and trained them for 16 weeks using a cycle ergometer, beginning 12 to 15 weeks after their first MI (myocardial infarction - a heart attack). Coital heart rate was measured twice before and twice after the training using a portable ECG recorder. Peak heart rate was 127 bpm before the training, and 120 bpm after training. In the control group of 6 men who did not train, peak heart rate remained statistically unchanged at 128 bpm.

• B.F. Skinner, in his summary of dozens of research studies, put it this way, "Looking at all of the studies on middle-aged men with or without MI, it is obvious that peak HR rarely exceeds 130-140 bpm. The relatively short period of peak intensity

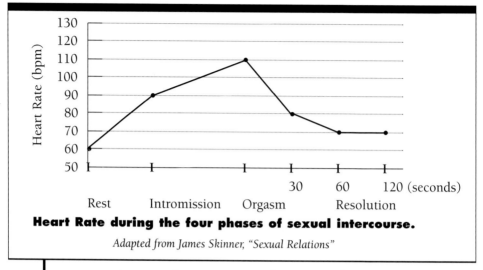

Heart Rate during the four phases of sexual intercourse.

Adapted from James Skinner, "Sexual Relations"

suggests that sexual intercourse in this group of men is not a strenuous activity."

As we mentioned before, very little research has been conducted on women. This is unfortunate, but what is available includes the following:

• Bartlett studied young women and found that heart rate during coitus was not very different from that of their male partners.

• Garcia-Barreto studied 13 men and 10 women who had previously experienced heart attacks. Using ECG monitoring, Garcia-Barreto found no significant differences between male and female patients at the time of orgasm after their heart complications, with men averaging 111 bpm and women, 104 bpm.

SEX IN SICKNESS AND IN HEALTH

Death from heart attacks during sexual activity seems to be another one of those myths that needs busting.

• Ueno, who reported on 5,559 sudden deaths in Japan, found that only 34 people (less than 1%) were engaged in sexual activity at the time of death. Of those, 80% were committing extramarital sex, and most were with partners 20 years younger, eating rich food, and drinking alcohol within hours before their deaths.

• Scheingold and Wagner suggests there might be an issue of familiarity with your partner. In their research, men having sex with a new partner had significantly higher heart rates and blood pressure values.

• Johnston reported on 10 cardiac patients who had sexual intercourse with someone other than their regular partners. Two of these patients felt that their angina or chest pain was more severe during intercourse with the new person.

It appears from these studies that there is a low incidence of death related to coitus at home with a spouse. It also appears that being a man away from home having sex with a younger woman, drinking and eating in excess, combined with the psychological pressures of guilt, possible fear of impotence and being caught, may have just been too much stress - it did them in.

We conclude that sex does not appear to be a high-risk activity for the majority of the population from a cardiovascular viewpoint.

For post-coronary patients, it appears that most should be able to perform satisfactorily sexually and that the psychological and emotional effects of a heart condition seem to be more significant than the physiological effects. It might be wise, though, for someone with cardiovascular limitations who undertakes a sexual relationship with a new person to be told of the possibility of increased heart rate response.

The bottom line is that the facts suggest sex is a Healthy Heart zone activity, and rarely does it take you up even to the Temperate zone! If your perception is that you are Redlining when you are in bed with your partner, slip on a chest strap and measure your heart rate yourself. But, be prepared for a Healthy Heart zone workout of less than 20 minutes in duration, which doesn't meet the ACSM guidelines for even minimum exercise intensity or time.

Most of all, have fun testing your own individual heart rate responses. In your testing experience, if you have data to share that would enhance the current available research, by all means fax or mail this information to me, and I'll spread the word with or without your name-your choice.

After lecturing to a group from the Specialized bike company on the material in this chapter, I made the same offer. One of the leaders in the group, who obviously listened intently and wanted his own research data, faxed me the next day a print-out from his heart rate monitor after he had downloaded just such an experience. He wrote in large letters "Woman on Top" and circled the highest heart rate number. Sure enough, the researchers were right - 110 bpm was his highest value.

Workout #12:
RATE NOT PACE WORKOUT

Purpose. The purpose of this workout is to learn the relationship between pace and heart rate (HR).

Introduction. Every time I hear timers calling out my minute-per-mile pace when I run, I use their cue to remind me that I need to listen to my heart rate monitor and not to them. The primary reason not to use pace or bike speed or other external data cues, is that it doesn't relate to any personally quantifiable data.

What happens to your pace when the temperature increases 15 degrees, when you hit the hills on the course, when there is shade, when you missed the aid station or when your blood glucose levels drop? Your heart rate monitor will quantify your physiological responses to the various racing stresses in real time, while the best the race clock can do is give you an elapsed time from which you can determine your after-the-fact average pace.

I have been using my heart monitor for the past 15 years and I am still surprised by the difference between what I feel about my pace or rate and the actual. My recommendation is that you train both systems - time and HR. Here's a great workout to do just that.

Workout. Find a measured course with mile markers. After a warm-up, do five one-mile repeats (5 x 1). Run at a steady pace with no accelerations. Each mile should be 30 seconds faster than the pace before and take at least two minutes active rest between each repeat. Always warm down at the end of the workout.

After the workout, average your HR for each of the one mile intervals by noting it for the last half mile or measuring it if you have this feature in your heart watch. Also note the corresponding training zone for your Max HR and your pace.

An example of what you need to record is shown below.

SAMPLE WORKOUT LOG

MILE PACE RUNNING	AVERAGE HR	TRAINING ZONES
9 min/mile	145 bpm	Middle Aerobic Zone
8.5 min/mile	151 bpm	Upper Aerobic Zone
8 min/mile	158 bpm	Lower Threshold Zone
7.5 min/mile	163 bpm	Middle Threshold Zone
7 min/mil	172 bpm	Upper Threshold Zone

Conclusion. You can now use the numbers from your "Rate Not Pace" workout to better understand the training zones they represent. When someone says to me, "Let's go for a five-mile run at about 8 minutes per mile pace," I always retort, "What about a five-miler in my lower Threshold Zone or about 160 bpm rate, not pace?"

Do this workout once a month because as your fitness improves, your average heart rate will drop. In other words, it will take less effort to run the same pace.

The Biofeedback Monitor:
Mind/Body

CHAPTER 17

BIOFEEDBACK

One of the fastest growing segments in sports performance is psychobiology, the study of mind-body relationships. One way of interpreting studies of psychobiology is to look at information gathered from biofeedback.

Getting feedback is developed by learning how to get the essential information needed to keep your efforts on track. Feedback essentially means the exchange of data about how one part of a system is working with the understanding that one part affects all others in the system. This exchange of information is like circulation, the lifeblood of your performance. Without feedback, we are in the dark as to how well we are doing. That's just what heart rate measurement is; it's the biofeedback or the information that you need to have as to how much stress you are experiencing in response to a condition.

The Two Minds

When the author Antonine de Saint-Exupery in *The Little Prince* wrote, "It is with the heart that one sees rightly; what is essential is invisible to the eye," he was saying that it's not just the mind's eye that is wise, it's the heart, the second mind, that is sometimes smarter. The heart muscle has become known as the seat of emotions. As such, if we can measure its activity we can measure our deepest feelings, our passions and longings and use them as a guide. When and why do we choose heart over head?

Sociobiologists have indicated that evolutionarily emotions have developed as a central role in our human psyche. Our emotions, they say, guide us in flight or fight decisions that can save our lives in times of danger. In terms of evolutionary history, these types of emotions have become necessary for their survival value and have become permanently a part of the reaction of the heart to stress and to relaxation.

As such, emotions then prepare the body for different kinds of responses. Here are the four major categories of the hundreds of different kinds of emotions that can be measured by a heart rate response:

* Anger. Heart rate increases and a rush of hormones, such as adrenaline, generates a pulse of energy strong enough for vigorous action. Blood flows to the hands in anger. Types of anger: fury, outrage, resentment, wrath, exasperation, indignation, acrimony, animosity, annoyance, irritability, hostility, and at the extreme, pathological hatred and violence.

* Fear. At the time that it hits, the body freezes for a moment and then circuits in the brain's emotional centres initiate a flood of hormones that put the body on a general alert, ready for action. Often you can feel your heart pounding in your chest as it speeds up. Blood pressure increases as blood flows to the large skeletal muscles, such as in the legs, making it easier to flee and making the face color ashen as blood is shunted away from it (sometimes creating the feeling that the "blood runs cold"). Other physiological responses to fear include heart rate increases, slow breathing, facial expressions, edginess. Types of fear include anxiety, apprehension, nervousness, concern, consternation, wariness, qualm, edginess, fright, terror, dread, and as a psycho-pathology; phobia and panic.

* Happiness. The brain centre inhibits negative feelings and increases energy as it quiets worrisome thoughts. The physiological change is that of quiescence which results in the body recovering more quickly from the biological arousal of upsetting emotions. Generally, heart rate drops as a body generally responds restfully. Types of happiness may include enjoyment, relief, joy, contentment, bliss, delight, amusement, pride, sensual pleasure, thrill, rapture, gratification, satisfaction, euphoria, whimsy, ecstasy, and at the extreme, mania.

* Love. This emotion is the physiological opposite of the "fight-or-flight" response shared by fear and anger. The nervous system responds with a "relaxation response" which consists of a set of body reactions that generate a general state of calm and contentment with the feeling of tenderness. Emotional terms that share love include acceptance, friendliness, trust, kindness, affinity, devotion, adoration, infatuation, agape.

Basically, there are two different ways of knowing: knowing with the heart which is the emotional mind impulsive and intuitive and knowing with the rational mind, the one that is thoughtful and powerful. In folk distinction there is a dichotomy between the "heart" and the "head." Knowing something is right "in your heart" and knowing it is right "in your mind" are two different ways of knowing. These two minds, the emotional and the rational, principally operate in close harmony. Even though they are semi-independent, there is a changing ratio of rational-to-emotional control over decisions. Feelings are essential to thought, thought is essential to feelings. But there are some emotions such as passion which ,when it surges, tips the balance and the emotional mind overtakes the rational mind. It can be so strong that "emotional hijacking" occurs.

Emotional hijacking is an emotional explosion which can range from when you feel like you "lost it" or blew up at someone to a degree of severity that you were so possessed by your emotions that you can't even remember what came over you. This is a form of neural hijacking.

So psychobiologists refer to this condition as "flooding" and the degree of it is measured in 10 beat heart rate increments above your ambient heart rate. If you are experienc-

ing flooding, and the heart rate reaches 100 bpm as it easily does when in rage or tears when your endocrine system is pumping adrenaline and other hormones that alert your physiology to the severity of the distress. The exact moment of an emotional hijacking is apparent from a heart rate jump often to as great as 30 bpm within the space of a heartbeat. Muscles tense; it can seem hard to breathe. At full hijacking there is a swamp of toxic feelings that are inescapable.

Knowing that flooding begins at 10 bpm, use your heart rate monitor to measure your emotional responses to different situations. Adjust for the situation. Call a time-out or take a 10 minute break or change the pace of the game. This is called playing to your emotional IQ rather than your intellectual IQ. They are two different quotients and they are both involved in performance and achievement. That's what sport hearts do.

ANTICIPATORY HEART RATE STATE

For all performance, we can determine a state of your rational mind and a state of your emotional mind. Just in advance of an event, we can set an anticipatory state of readiness. This is often called the "ideal state of excitability," and it can be measured by using heart rate and measuring what is called "anticipatory heart rate." The energy elicited from this state of excitability can be harnessed and become a positive or a negative motivator. If the anxiety gets too high or if the excitement is too low, you'll see a diminished performance. The classic research in this area of performance describes the relationship between excitement and performance in terms of an upside-down U. At the top of the inverted U is the optimal relationship between anticipatory anxiety and performance. But, too little excitement - the first side of the U - results in apathy or too low a motivational excitement, while too much anxiety - the other side of the U - sabotages our performance. Look at the graph that follows to understand the relationship between physical performance and emotional pre-event excitability.

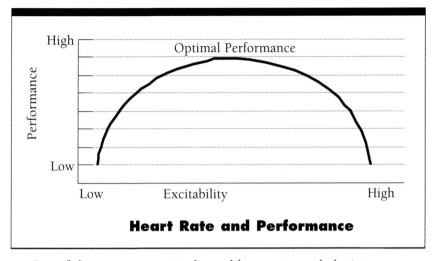

Heart Rate and Performance

One of the measurement tools used by sports psychologists to predict an ideal performance state is heart rate. This anticipatory heart rate varies among sports and individuals, depending on the demands of the activity and level of excitement. For you to determine your pre-event ideal anticipatory heart rate, you will need to do your own self-analysis and in part, note your individual responses in different situations and begin to assess your patterns of readiness.

A good example of this psychobiological relationship is shown in the results from studies completed on elite level shooters - pistol and rifle. Heart rate response was measured in a number of ways such as where the shot occurred in the cardiac cycle, cardiac deceleration, respiration, electroencephalographic (EEG) recordings and other measures. The results (Daniel Landers, *Psychophysiological Assessment and Biofeedback*) reveal the importance of the mind-body connection with regards to heart rate.

In their study, the average heart rate for the shooters before they shot was 73.3 bpm. Average heart rate during shooting was 86.3 bpm or a 13 bpm increase. Heart rate increases in a sports activity which has limited increases in cardiac requirements because of the arousal level of the shooter. Those in the study (sample size 62, male and female rifle/pistol shooters) whose heart rate dropped below resting or increased more than 50 beats above resting during their shooting period, scored the worst. The best shooters were those whose heart rate increased between 8-50 bpm. This means that for most shooters, there is an individualised optimal performance state that can be measured by heart rate monitoring.

When presented in graph form, the research showed that the inverted U relationship between heart rate and performance optimized at a heart rate of 92.6. This heart rate - 92.6 bpm - was the best indicator of shooting performance. From this graph, you can see that shooters perform better with heart rate elevated to an optimal level. It's important to know that the optimal heart rate for each individual shooter varies. Knowing these ideal performance heart rate ranges can be useful in providing feedback to any athlete. As a side note, it was thought by many shooters that the most desirable time to fire the pistol/rifle was between heartbeats. In fact, the researchers showed that there was no consistency in pulling the trigger in relationship to the cardiac cycle.

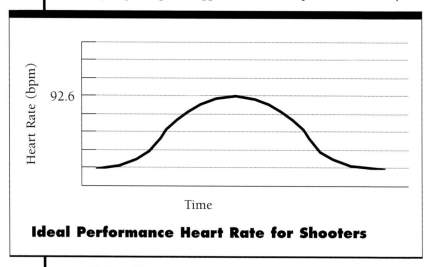

Ideal Performance Heart Rate for Shooters

ANGER AND HEART FUNCTION

Of all of the different emotions measured, anger was the only one which resulted in a drop in cardiac efficiency. That is, heart rate increases but stroke volume decreases. From dozens of studies to date, all the findings demonstrate the power of anger to damage the heart. Anger leads to higher cardiac risk for those who display it. It appears that anger and hostility may be one of the causes of the early development of coronary artery disease and that it may intensify the problem once heart disease has begun.

Physiologically, the stress from each episode of anger results in increasing heart rate and blood pressure. When these episodes become chronic whether the anger is expressed or not, then cardiac risk is dramatically increased. The good news is that chronic anger need not be a death sentence. You can change habits, and hostility is one habit that can change with help. The antidote to anger and hostility is to develop a trusting heart. With the right training and using a heart rate monitor as a biofeedback tool, hostility can be diminished. As people realise that anger can lead to an early grave, monitoring anger becomes more critically important.

Unburdening a troubled, a heavy, an angry, a depressed heart appears to be good medicine.

MONITORING YOUR EMOTIONS

Your coach and friend, the heart rate monitor, is the best tool we have available today to help you learn how to read and control your emotions. A smart heart uses this tool because its emotional intelligence (EQ) is as much if not more important than mental intelligence (IQ). Emotional intelligence comes from mastery of your emotional intellect.

As author and psychologist James Loehr writes in *The Mental Game,* "If you are aware of the times when your fighting spirit is apt to desert you, and if you can harness your intensity and confidence, you'll have a distinct advantage over the player who allows his (her) emotions to manipulate him (her)." Intensity and harnessing the power of intensity can lead to accomplishing your goals and it can be measured by using your monitor to assess your physiological response to the moment.

Let's use an example of strong EQ talent. Say you are running in a 10K race and your best friend catches you and passes you. You thought you were in better shape than your friend but maybe it's not your day; your biorhythms are down. Then you experience the "letdown" phenomenon of mentally and physically letting your competitors pull away from you as you suffer defeat, personal and actual. If we plotted your heart rate response during this scene, we probably would see a dramatic drop in your heart rate, or under arousal, after you were beaten by your emotional response.

Letting down in a competition of any kind is a mental state of under activation or low arousal response. That is, you are not sufficiently aroused to perform at your best. In heart zone training terms, it's loss of heart rate intensity and can be measured by a lowering of heart rate, blood pressure, and other biochemical changes. In fact, you are not performing as well because you are not producing enough mental energy to do so. You suddenly don't try as hard, you lack that motivation or fight-response, and the result is impaired performance.

It's frequently seen in the game of tennis. Watch as a player is ahead and all of a sudden their momentum falters. It seems as if they run out of steam and lose consistently. This sudden drop of performance or state of under activation can be traced in this

example to a number of factors. According to Loehr, "Some players are incredible fighters. They're always coming at you whether ahead or behind, playing well or poorly, they're like bloodhounds on a hot scent. Adverse conditions, bad luck, and unfair calls rarely dampen their spirit. They consistently overcome these obstacles with two emotional responses: they become challenged and remarkably persistent." This is one of the smart heart's successful styles.

The emotional response opposite to under arousal is over activation. In this case of high nervousness, the athlete is trying too hard, is too excited or too angry or, if we used a car engine as an analogy, their rpms are too high. At the start of a race you'll frequently see a runner take off like a rabbit, only to later fade because they "went out too fast." Indeed, they did that probably because their arousal was so high and their perceived speed or intensity was low. Monitoring heart rate can abate that rabbit phenomenon. When your heart rate numbers drop uncharacteristically during or after a game or event, you are usually experiencing the letdown phenomenon. When heart rate numbers which stay uncharacteristically high during a recovery period are not attributable to exertion, they indicate over arousal.

At mile 23 in the marathon of one of the hardest races in the world, the Ironman Triathlon, I caught and passed my nemesis, the woman who was in first place in the master's division. I looked at my monitor, and after 10 hours of racing, it was at that moment of intense arousal reading 186 bpm (my Max HR is 192). I had two miles to go to the finish line and I couldn't afford to "letdown" or I'd lose. I raced with all heart and total fatigue for those last miles. For one of the few times in my life, I experienced what is the highest feeling in an athlete's life, the "ideal performance state," and though it was an extreme level of exertion, it was effortless. I was zoned, I was maxed out, I was hazed-tranced-psyched-pumped-tranced. I was in complete and exhilarating flow. I won the race, and crossing that finish line and looking up at the finish clock is a feeling and moment that is frozen in time for me. I felt a profound inner stillness and well-being. It was joy, power, control in one. Clearly, my mental state at this moment was my zenith and dramatically different from the mental state of poor performance. At that moment when I passed her, I have to confess I threw away my heart rate monitor (well, it was so high at 186 bpm anyway) and I ran to win. I ran these last few miles and I ran because it was effortless. This was one of my peak athletic moments, this was truly the ideal performance state.

EMOTIONAL AND PHYSICAL ZONING

To trigger this ideal performance state is not the result of athletically playing well; rather you play well because you are in the zone. This is an important distinction. Zoning is a state of emotional balance. When your emotions change, your biochemistry changes. When your biochemistry changes, so changes your performance. It's when the chemistry and the mind are in balance, when there is a rich mixture of the mind and the body that you achieve maximal performance.

The zone is actually a fine-tuned place, it's not a chemically induced trance state. And it's controlled by you. You create the state of mind-body where your emotional and mental climate is maximised. As you practice this technique, watch the changes in your heart rate's response to our different mind-body situations. Zoning is a learned state and there are a few ways to practice getting into your ideal performance zone:

• *Positive Mind-Emotion State.* Listen to your positive inner self-talk, think positively, talk positively, look for the good and strong in yourself and your performance. This positive emotional methodology will increase your body's chemistry to provide the emotional and spiritual fuel for performance. Replace anger with challenge, fear with desire, frustration with determination, and each time you will be learning how to program your mental zone.

• *Enhanced Self Awareness.* Fine tune your awareness by feeling the mental and emotional state when you are successful. What is your mental and emotional climate during your best athletic moments? When you get into flow, what does it feel like and how did you get there? Learning how to become more self aware leads to opening the pathways to more self awareness.

• *Combining Mental Zone and Physical Zone.* As you learn the never-ending process of zoning, observe the differences between when you are only mentally or only physically in the performance state. It's by the combination of the two that you reach your highest state. The blocks to physical zoning can be anything from overtraining, to dietary problems, lack of real sleep, and muscle imbalance, while the blocks to mental zoning can be emotions, concentration, or self esteem. Unless the blocks are released, unless the two, EQ and IQ can merge, only then can you achieve optimally.

• *Positive Visualisation*. Creating a positive image of your actions and feelings leads to their outcome. If you are a triathlete, visualising passing riders on their bikes is positive visualisation. Visualising not being passed on the bike, or not going down on your bike, or not having a mechanical breakdown is negative visualisation. What you most fear too often becomes true because your mind cannot tell the difference easily between a real visual cue and an imagined one. Clearly, if you are not winning or achieving your goal, something is breaking down. Understanding these breakdowns is the first step to improvement. That's how you turn a breakdown into a breakthrough.

ATHLETIC STRESS

Exercise deals with both of the two kinds of basic stress: emotional and physical. Both can be measured by their biochemical responses. A heart rate monitor is a personal power tool because it can measure biochemical changes. Stress can also be classified as external and internal. Heat, altitude, lack of sleep, nutrient changes are all types of external stress. Anger, anxiety, fear, happiness are a few of the internal stresses that we encounter.

Managed stress in the right amount is healthy for us. That's because the body adapts to positive stress by getting stronger and fitter, to negative stress by getting weaker and deconditioned. This process is called "adaptation" and it's why we expose the body to exercise stress - to enhance its ability to do work. If we apply too much exercise stress, the adaptation that occurs is called "overtraining" and if we apply not enough stress, then we are under training the body and mind.

Sports training is a form of physical and emotional stress in a controlled dose which leads to improvements in our strength, flexibility and cardiovascular capacity. Races, tournaments, and meets are all examples of emotional stress, which managed and controlled, leads to improvements in our mental strength, flexibility, and fitness.

Perception of an event is a key to the dimension of the stress. If you perceive something as threatening, then it will be an increased stressor. If you perceive the same event as enjoyable, then it will be less stressful.

Exposure to high amounts of stress leads to burnout. Racing too much can lead to temporary mental burnout, while training in too high a zone for too much time in zone can lead to a temporary physical burnout. Too much time in the athletic pressure cooker - too much training and racing - can lead to permanent burnout.

Recovery is a key antidote to stress. Recovery is that time when we are relaxed and rid of stressors. There are both mental and physical components to recovery and both types are required for full recovery. Recovery can be easily measured using heart rate technology and logging your exercises. When rapid heart rate recovery occurs, both mental and physical stress is at its lowest. Active recovery means that the physical stress of high intensity is removed but the person remains active and does not sit or lie down for recovery.

How fast you recover is an indicator of stress reduction competence. For example, when I swim in my redline zone (Max HR swim 170 bpm) and do repeat intervals at 155 bpm, if I completely rest between intervals I usually see my heart rate drop a beat per second. If I notice after 30 seconds that my heart rate has only dropped 20 beats, I know that this is not a characteristic recovery rate and that I am not recovering as fully as normal. I then adjust my workout to lower the stress level.

Similarly, if I see that my morning resting heart rate is more than about 5 bpm higher than its characteristic value, I know I am over-stressed and I change my entire day's activities. This resting measurement is telling me that I am in a higher than normal stressed condition which is a response to some biochemical activity within me. When I ignore this information, inevitably my day goes poorly with high expectations that are not met, with the onset of a problem whether mental or physical, and without my normal energy level.

Just as there are chemical changes in the muscle tissue which causes a muscle to contract (known as the Kreb's cycle), so there are chemical changes that happen from the mind sending transmitters which result in the emotions changing. Credit for this discovery goes in large part to Chadace Pert, formerly chief of brain biochemistry at the National Institute of Mental Health. After years of research, she discovered "neuropeptides", which are small protein-like chemicals housed in the brain's limbic system and are the transmitters of emotions and feelings. The limbic system which has long been known as the emotional centre within the brain, controls the chemicals - neurohormones such as catecholamines - that cause emotional change.

These chemicals are the mind's response to stress and relaxation. To increase your ability to recover from stress, improvement in neurohormonal function is necessary. This is accomplished most healthily by living a life of balanced stress and recovery, by expending and recapturing personal energy. This process is one example of "oscillation" or wave theory.

Living things oscillate. Dead things don't oscillate. To live is to pulsate and to not-live is to cease oscillating. Pulsation creates waves such as in heart waves (EKG), muscle waves (EMG), and brain waves (EEG). The wave-energy theory has been popularised by Irv Dardik, M.D., sprinter, former vascular surgeon now in private practice and founder of the USOC's Sports Medicine Council. Dardik uses heart zone training with his patients to get them healthier by having them oscillate in and out of high and low zones. When at the cellular level, the cell pulsates rhythmically as a response to the oscillation between stress and recovery, the heart gets healthier. This energy-wave theory, according to Dardik, can lead to the reversal of disease and to restoration of health among the sick. Too much oscillation without recovery leads to a breakdown in our immune system's ability to fight against disease. Rather, health is a balanced cycle of stress and recovery which stabilises the body's delicate bio and neurochemical responses.

Meanwhile, sport psychologist James Loehr in his book *Toughness Training for Life* applies the same wave theory principles as he "discovered the powerful role balanced stress and recovery play in the mental toughening process."

Some of Loehr's research dealt with "between point recovery" time for professional tennis players. Since 85% of the total time in a tennis match is between points, it's key that players learn to use this time to maximise their 15% of the time offensively and defensively during point playing of the game. Sure enough, poor tennis players were not as disciplined, less ritualistic, had more variety in their actions, and were less exact during the between-point time. These same individuals experience more difficulty in recovering between points. Loehr strapped a heart rate monitor chest strap on them and measured the changes in their heart rate during practice and game situations. He discovered that when they performed well, their heart rate pattern was wave-like, not linear and flat. He discovered that waves of stress were followed by waves of recovery and that the two waves were symmetrical. For the poor performers, there were no waves; their heart rate was linear. When he taught the poor performers to create symmetrical stress and recovery waves, their performance improved dramatically.

His point is that this phenomenon applies to our everyday life. We need symmetrical waves of during-point stress which is *stress at work* and between-point time as *recovery as non-work*. Life and sports have numerous parallels and stress recovery is one of those. In life, exercise is sometimes thought of as not productive and sometimes as non important non-work time. Rather, viewed in this light, it is critical to keep us oscillating to improve our immune system, to keep us in balance. Just as the between-point recovery period is key for success in tennis, so does our personal recovery time - relaxation and recuperation - provide us with a greater capacity for energy expenditure and happiness.

Here's an example. We have three staff members on a team. The first, Suzan, likes to work at her desk with few breaks and eats lunch at her desk. Tom, on the other hand, likes to go to the break room and hang out. Meanwhile, Kathy, who is the highest producer and has been promoted numerous times likes to get up from her desk every hour and walk for five minutes. She walks about one lap around the office building stopping by the water cooler for a drink. What happens to the pulsation wave-energy to these three individuals?

Suzan is an over trainer and is constantly in stress with linearity and little to no oscillation in her day. She's a candidate for ulcers. Tom under trains and spends too much time in relaxation and eventually was fired for not producing. And finally, Kathy, at the end of the day, has high energy and is cheerful and will continue to be promoted for being effective and probably live a long life.

The point is that living a balanced and productive emotional and physical life means that we need to experience periods of stress and recovery that is healthy and has spikes and troughs, valleys and mountains. The next time someone says, "Give me a break," don't use it as a throwaway line, but take a break with them because it is a wave or recovery time to get you out of your linearity mode.

Some think that stress kills us. It may. However, high doses of stress can be helpful and provide for adaptation to occur if there is a sufficient wave of recovery to accommodate it. Stress won't break you unless you fail to plan for sufficient recovery. High linear stress, for example, in the form of a high ambient or resting heart rate or feeling like you are in a high pressure environment continuously can be lethal. But high wave-energy stress can be healthy with relief in the form of healthy recovery.

The human being is one of the most awesome cyber-machines to ever stalk the planet. Martial arts master and exercise theorist George Leonard perhaps put it best when he wrote that we are all mostly unrealized potential. When we thrill to an event like the Olympics, we're not responding to whose training regimen was the best or which country had the best nutritionist. Instead, we resonate to people who grasp a small part of that potential and *reach*. It is the reach that's important. I have been lucky enough to stand at the starting lines with great athletes, and I have been privileged to make whatever small marks I've made. But what I have come to learn is that the reach is more important than the grasp.

WORKOUT #15:
THE BODY-MIND SESSION

Introduction. The heart muscle has a dual role: to be a blood pump and to be the mental inspiration pump. With the emphasis today on the mind-body connection or psychobiology, one can easily see that the heart is a double muscle. It provides for both work capacity and for mental desire. Here's a workout that challenges both of the heart's primary capacities - a mind-body connector.

Purpose. To measure your ability to accurately predict heart rates during varying paces.

Workout Plan. Set your heart rate monitor so the alarm sounds every 10 minutes. You will have to use your wrist watch if your model does not have this feature. Calculate and post 70 percent of your max heart rate (Max HR) and each five percent increase up to 90 percent. If you don't know your max, take a test. For a Max HR of 195 beats per minute (bpm) these values would be 137, 146, 156, 165 and 175 bpm.

Workout. Warm-up for however long is appropriate for your selected activity then begin your workout and start the alarm function on your watch or monitor. Without looking at your monitor, workout for 10 minutes at what you think or perceive to be 70 percent of your Max HR. Exert a steady-state effort for the entire 10 minutes.

When the alarm sounds, look at the monitor and make a mental or physical note of the HR. Step up the interval (this is a 10-minute ladder) to what you think is 75 percent of max for 10 minutes without looking at the monitor. When the alarm sounds, note the actual HR and keep a mental record of it. If you can do the math, note your error.

Follow the same procedure for 80 percent, and 85 percent if you can maintain it. If this pace is above your anaerobic threshold HR, you probably cannot withstand it. Warm down, then compare your perceived effort with your actual HR. The error may be so great that you may never train without a monitor again.

Outcome. If you are more than five beats off, you need to train your mind more than your body to truly and undeniably know (and I use the word "know" as in having knowledge) your HR intensity.

Repeatedly to ad nauseam, I hear people say, "I don't need a heart rate monitor because I know my HR whenever I train." This is athletic elitism and arrogance at its most obvious.

After completing this workout, I "know" that you will agree that my friend and Olympic Biathlete Lyle Nelson is right when he writes, "It takes a lot of heart (blood pumping capacity) and a lot of "heart" (confidence and inspiration) to achieve your best-possible performance. It's only with the heart rate monitor that you can achieve both. I "know" and I "feel". This is the mind-body connection." (*The Fitness Monitor Newsletter*).

Every Heart
& Every Body

We sit across the conference table from each other, separated by gulfs of hardwood and culture. The four Japanese businessmen in their dark suits and white shirts smile politely, looking directly at my more informal team of three.

We've come to this conference table to try to effect an unlikely alliance, marrying our very American franchise of athletic footwear specialty stories to the very Japanese monolith of one of the semi-legendary billion-billion yen *kegetsu* conglomerates. Their business is the business of international commerce, the pouring of molten steel, the creation of silicon chips- not the business of running and athletic shoes-with an annual report that looks like a telephone book.

We've done our homework on these gentlemen, and frankly, we are more than a little puzzled. Finally, we decide that I should open the meeting in classic American cowgirl - blunt - style: "Why would a *kegetsu* be interested in having the Japanese rights to a small American franchise company?"

There is a slight, perhaps not entirely comfortable, pause. Then the most senior representative, with carefully selected and placed words, explains that it is not necessarily the company they covet. What they would like to import, rather, is our values.

It would give their company great status, he continues, if they could bring to Japan a company like ours, a "be" company.

"Our society has historically been one of spectators," he says. "Those who watch and don't do. But we are trying to become a society of participants - those who do and want to become. We would, ultimately, like to evolve into the highest state, that of being fit and strong, living our values by being who we are and living a fitness lifestyle."

Watch…do…be.

What this monument of Japanese, no, *world* business wanted to buy from us was a promissory note, a note that says each of us can evolve through the different stages of watch/do/be. We wanted to sell him this note, but with the understanding that change takes time. There's no quick repay-ment plan. But he was right - our little company has a lifestyle that works, that delivers on that evolutionary promise.

Watch…do…be. Wherever you are on that never-ending cycle, Heart Zone Training, a revolutionary new fitness, health, performance, and weight management system, is the program that can help you translate your goals into reality and, ultimately, into the healthy and nurturing lifestyle. This isn't a "talk-show" miracle. We don't have pills that can make you be thinner, richer, smarter, and more attractive. Rather, here is something based on scientific foundations that's guaranteed to work.

What we do have is a plan - a system - we call Heart Zone Training, that can free you from *watching* (whether it's a video your eyes are glued to or this book) and lead you through *doing* to the highest stage, *being*. It doesn't matter where you place yourself on the continuum from couch potato to Olympian; Heart Zone Training is a personal fitness revolution that can and will work for you. The point of the story and Heart Zone Training is that we have a credible chance of reaching fulfilment, of living happiness if we can transcend into a lifestyle of health and fitness. "Being" in the watch…do…be progression is when you accomplish that.

You've probably heard that word "revolution" before, attached to everything from exercise machines to chips and dip. We think, though, we've really got something here. The revolu-tionary secret behind Heart Zone Training is the soul of a new machine: the heart rate monitor. A heart rate monitor does exactly what it sounds like it should be doing - monitoring your heart rate. Technology has evolved to the point where any of us can put a band with a transmitter around our chests, then watch our hearts thump…thump…thump on the watch-like receiver on our wrists.

So, what's so revolutionary about this?

Just this: for the first time we have a solid link between our bodies and our minds, a reliable feedback loop that connects the brains with the brawn, so that we are truly *in control* of our bodies' training. That's what *Heart Zone Training* is.

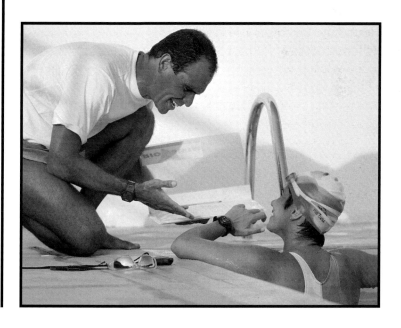

Questions & Answers

Question: If your heart rate increases during exercise does it mean that energy expenditure is also increasing:

Answer: No. Heart rate increase and energy expenditure increase are not the same. For example, you might think that as heart rate increases so does the number of calories per hour that you are spending at that given time. In fact, that's not the case. In aerobic dance, when you lift your hands and arms overhead in one of the typical dance sequences, heart rate increases but VO_2 expenditure or energy expenditure does not increase. Heart rate is used as a way to roughly measure increases in energy expenditure but it's not always directly related.

Here's another example. You run for thirty minutes and your average heart rate for the workout is, say, 150 bpm. Two days later you run the same thirty minutes and the ambient temperature has increased to over 90 degrees and your heart rate is now 160 bpm. Did you run faster? Did you burn more calories because your heart rate was higher?

Rather, your heart rate increased as a way for the body to circulate more blood to your skin as a cooling mechanism - your muscles aren't burning any more calories to run. Likewise, your heart rate increases with aerobic dancing to pump blood against more peripheral resistance of your hands being higher than the height of your heart.

In fact, your heart has to pump at a higher rate to increase the cardiac output. The cardiac law states that CO must remain constant so HR increases and SV increases when workload increases

The real point is that you want to measure energy expenditure as that's really the best way to measure how much work or exercise you are experiencing. Since it's expensive and difficult to put gas analysers and lactate analysers on everyone in an aerobics class, it's easier to use heart rate as a nearly-as-good measurement method of energy expenditure.

Question: Are Peak Heart Rate and Max Heart Rate the same?
Answer: No, peak heart rate is the highest heart rate number you experience during any single exercise bout while Max HR is your sport specific individually and genetically determined highest number of beats per minute that your heart can beat.

Question: If max HR declines for those who have remained unfit, is it a direct, longitudinal decline.
Answer: No. It seems that max HR declines in the unfit population but it's not equivalent to one beat for each year you get older. Rather, it seems to decline more quickly in your older years than in your younger years. For the unfits, the decline should more resemble this graph than the one you may have seen in textbooks:

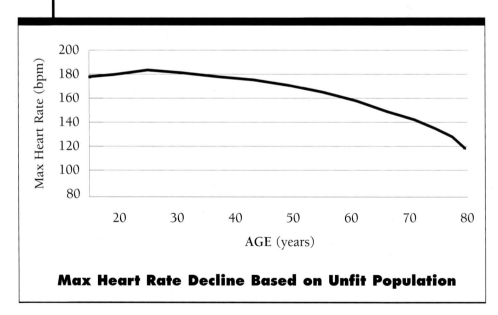

Max Heart Rate Decline Based on Unfit Population

Question: Is clinical maximum heart rate the same as absolute maximum heart rate?

Answer: No. If you have your max measured at a lab or on a piece of exercise equipment, it may test differently than when you reach max actually doing the activity. That's what absolute max is – it's your true, doing it in the specific activity, heart rate. As an example, let's say you measure your max HR on a stationary bike indoors, this is your "clinical max". Then, you take your road bike and go out on a slight and long incline and test it in the field. The two numbers are different. The latter, on your bike, should be higher, and that should be your absolute maximum heart rate.

Tips About Your HR Monitor

Every model and manufacturer has a different "update time." Update time is the number of seconds between readings on your monitor. It's usually 3-5 seconds between each time period when you'll have a new number on your monitor, which means that it has updated you to your next heart rate level. The faster the update usually the better because the information more accurately reflects your changes in intensity.

•Irregular numbers. Whenever my monitor starts to act up and bouncing all over with numbers or errors, I usually look to my transmitter as the first cause of the problem. Moisten the electrodes on the chest strap to see if it's a conductivity problem then press on the transmitter to check that your chest strap is tight enough. It's rarely your receiver or watch unit that causes the problem unless a battery is fading. Look for exterior interference from another user or a radio tower, etc.

• The first few numbers are weird. The first few numbers you read on your monitor when you start it are usually wrong because it simply takes about sixty seconds for the algorithms to average enough sample numbers to be accurate. I just don't look at my watch for the first couple of minutes as I am stretching or warming up.

• Interference. There are several things which emit a lot of electromagnetic waves (EMG). So don't wear your heart rate monitor when you are travelling on an airplane or in a car. If you are on a piece of exercise equipment, move the monitor around until you can find an area where there is no interference.

• The dreaded "First Wind Phenomenon". You may notice an abrupt jump in your heart rate the first few minutes of exercise and then a gradual drop as you hold a steady state pace. This is called the "first wind" which, most concur, is a warm-up effect caused by changes in the fuels used by the muscles.

• Chest Problems. Some people have a concave shaped chest (especially bodybuilders) and a chest strap doesn't lie flat across their chest because of the hollow space. Try your transmitter unit on your back. They work well there.

The Cardiac Muscle Monitor

Do you want to know what makes our hearts tick? Are you curious as to exactly how heart rate monitors do their job? Well, you've come to the right place. It's not necessary to know the following technical details in order to get the benefits of heart-rate monitored training, but it can be fun trivia to share during your next training session with friends.

The Heart: Pumps and Polarizations

The basic idea most of us have about the heart is that it is a pump, but really it's two pumps, two sides, in one. Each pump or side of the heart has three valves: 1) *ingoing*, dividing the outside of the heart from the first, upper chamber, 2) *interior*, dividing the upper and lower chambers on each side from one another, and 3) *outgoing*, dividing the lower chamber from the outside of the heart.

The pump on the right side of the heart receives returning, or "venous," blood from all parts of the body. The first right-hand chamber (the right atrium) fills and then quickly passes about a cupful or so of blood with each stroke. The blood goes through the interior valve into the lower chamber (the right ventricle) which is much larger and more powerful. The right ventricle then ejects the blood up to the lungs for carbon dioxide off-loading and oxygen on-loading. The same cupful of blood returns from the lungs and enters the top half of the left-side pump – the left atrium. The heart takes a brief rest while the atrium fills – it takes time for the muscle to contract and eject the blood. From the left atrium, the left interior valve passes the blood to the last chamber, the left ventricle, which is the largest

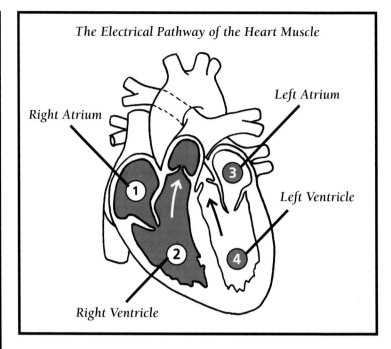

The Electrical Pathway of the Heart Muscle

of all of the heart chambers and which jettisons the blood out through the aorta, and from there to the rest of the body.

The coordination of two pumps, four chambers, and six valves is one of those wondrous activities of the nervous system, orchestrated via chemical transmitters and electrical impulses. Interestingly, most of the time the cardiac muscle is on its own. It independently creates its own electrical signals without any signals from the brain, rhythmically beating away until there's an order to make a change.

The communication signal for the cardiac muscle to contract begins at the sino-atrial (S-A) node. The S-A node independently and rhythmically sends out an electrical message from inside the upper part of the right atrium. This message instructs the atriums to contract, and they do so concurrently, ejecting blood down into the ventricles. This S-A message is the depolarisation phase of the upper chambers. As the message arrives at the doorstep of the atrial-ventricular node (A-V node) located on the inside of the same chamber and near the center of the heart muscle, the

A-V node sends out a second signal. This is the depolarisation of the ventricle muscles. The A-V node alerts the two bottom chambers, the ventricles, to contract. All of this is timed perfectly. After the upper two chambers contract, there is a delay of about 0.13 seconds for the message to be sent from the S-A to the A-V node. This timing is critical - it's the time the heart muscle uses to squeeze the blood out of the upper chambers and into the lower chambers.

The A-V node is a ball of special muscle cells that extend out of the right atrium like a lead wire running down the inside centre of the heart and breaking apart into branches (called Bundle branches). When the A-V node extension wire reaches the lower ventricle chambers, it branches again and then it branches some more until it permeates uniformly to the two lower chambers. This branching is important because it allows the message to travel quickly to all parts of the lower chambers, so that when the muscles contract, they do so as one unit and not sequentially. This allows for more complete expulsion of all of the blood from the chamber.

This contraction represents one heartbeat.

The Heart: Beats and Waves

Each heartbeat is one wave form that has a specific "healthy" shape when viewed on an electrocardiogram. The heartbeat is diagrammed into phases called the P-Q-R-S-T waves.

P Wave: The depolarisation and contraction of the atria.

Q-R-S Wave: The signal passing down the AV node, depolarisation and contraction of the ventricles.

T Wave: The repolarization of the ventricles.

A smaller wave, when the atria are repolarized, is hidden by the strength of the QRS complex - so it can't be seen in the wave form.

The waiting time (called a refractory period) for the heart to depolarize is important because it allows for the filling of the chambers and for the heart muscle to rest. If there weren't enough filling time, then not enough blood would enter the pumps and the cardiac output or amount of blood ejected would be insufficient. This is probably the reason your heart maxes out at some number of beats per minute - beyond the max there isn't enough filling time.

Heart rate monitors are not electrocardiographs. Heart rate monitors measure only the number of beats over a period of time. Electrocardiographs, however, measure the entire wave form of each heartbeat. As the heart rate increases, the wave form changes shape. For example, at high heart rates, the Q-T complex compresses and the amplitude or height of the R-wave decreases while the height of the Q-waves and T-waves increases. At slower heart rates the wave shape has a greater height or amplitude.

Resting ECG wave form

Exercise technologists and cardiologists use ECG printouts to screen for unhealthy hearts. If there is an abnormality, it will frequently be uncovered from a stress test with an ECG measurement. Where in the wave form the abnormality appears, leads specialists to determine the nature of the heart problem. For example, if the S-T part of the wave form is depressed and if the depolarisation of the ventricles is slow, that is an indication that there is not enough blood reaching the heart muscle (myocardial ischemia), which can result in damage to the heart muscle.

A measure of heartbeats is a heart rhythm, passing through its different polarized and depolarized phrases. It's this electric change that the ECG electrodes sense. As the process begins, positive ions spread across the cell membranes and depolarize the tissue. Then, there's a sudden change and a negative wave crosses over and the muscle contracts. This change from the positive to the negative state is called one heartbeat. This continuous process of depolarisation and repolarization causing contraction and relaxation of the cardiac muscle forms the basis of the heart rhythm.

There is a high incidence of abnormal heart rhythms among well-trained athletes. It's not clear why. Don't worry if you are one of these folks. Though normally this would be considered an indication of serious heart disease, researchers have concluded that in the absence of other symptoms, these variations in heart rhythms are normal and do not necessarily indicate any problem.

The Heart Rate Monitor: Electrodes

The electrical charge created from the polarization and depolarisation of the four chambers is conducted throughout the entire body via the body fluids to the skin surface. Electrodes are placed on the skin at locations on either side of the heart to pick up the positive charge and the change to a negative charge, and the electrodes measure the difference between them. The electrical charge from the heart muscle is extremely small so the equipment has to be extremely sensitive to detect it. The ECG wave form's most distinguishable portion is the QRS complex. The QRS complex has both the highest amplitude (measuring about 1 MV) and the fastest average frequency or time (about 20 HZ). This serves as the detectable wave form for all ECG heart rate monitors.

Now, the heart isn't unique in creating electrical charges when it contracts and relaxes; when *any* muscle contracts, there is electrical activity. So, telling the difference between your skeletal muscles contracting and your heart rate muscle contracting can be a problem. This is called muscle noise.

There are other reasons that getting a clear heart signal is tricky. For one, dry skin is not a good conductor. Wet skin is a problem, too, because this creates an "offset potential" (the reaction of perspiration with a conductive electrode to produce an electro-chemical-battery that generates voltage) between the skin and the electrode. The result is motion artifacts and signal noise. A motion artifact is caused by movement of the individual, which can cause movement of the electrodes' contacts and signal-distorting noise.

Luckily, there are some pretty good solutions to these problems caused by dry conductive electrodes - the only kind used presently on wireless portable heart rate monitors. First, the electrodes are placed over the heart area where the signal has the shortest distance to travel. By placing the sensing electrodes near the source of the signal it also ensures that the signal will have less distortion and greater amplitude. It also reduces the possibility of additional muscle noise.

To lessen the motion and pressure artifacts, the microprocessors inside the monitors are equipped with noise-processing software. This software is designed to distinguish between different signals that are not within the frequency and millivolt amplitude of the QRS complex signal. In other words, they throw out quirky signals that don't fit a certain scope.

The result is that your personal heart rate monitor is extremely good at what it does - counting your heart beats.

The Heart Rate Monitor Transmitter

The electrodes which pick up the impulses from your heart are generally mounted on a chest strap, and data is transmitted from the chest strap, usually to a receiver on your wrist, via one of three methods.

• EMG Telemetry: These are electromagnetic, radio-like waves. EMG's have an extremely low frequency that are telemetered to the receiving unit with a range of about 1.5 meters. This means your receiving unit should not be more than 3 feet away from its transmitter or it'll likely lose the signal. This is not a problem if you are wearing the receiver as a watch. You might notice that you get better information if you position the receiver in a certain alignment with the transmitter. That's because of signal direction and strength. Most have a strong signal directed forward but a weak backward signal. Some models of transmitters can be worn on your back and the radio waves can still be easily detected on the wrist. All transmitters and receivers are battery powered.

• Hard Wired: The data is transmitted to the receiver via a directly attached lead wire. This rather awkward method is used today only in clinical equipment.

• Infrared Transmission: The signal is sent to the receiver via light waves. This is usually the method when the receiving unit is a computer or is located on the control panel of exercise equipment.

The Heart Rate Monitor Receiver

The words "heart rate monitor" and "heart rate watch" are synonymous unless there isn't a timing function included in the receiving unit. Monitors are the receiving units that get the transmitted data from the chest strap and process it through an integrated circuit. The heart rate number they calculate is usually updated every 3-5 seconds if the monitor doesn't use real time. The first few numbers that appear on your watch should be tossed out because the monitor needs enough sample heart rates to calculate an accurate number. Likewise, if you quickly accelerate or decelerate, the monitor's displayed heart rate values will always be lagging behind your real heart rate numbers.

It's the signal processing software that does the mathematical calculation of beat-to-beat heart rate. Some manufacturers employ programming to reject artifact and non rhythmic inputs. Still others display a beat to beat average of heart rate with the artifact and noise filtered. The less sophisticated ones are using older technologies such as displaying long-running averages.

One of my favourite workouts is to strap sometimes as many as six different monitors on at the same time and compare the simultaneous readings. I look like a gypsy in lycra fabric as the watches run up and down my arms from my wrists to my elbows. I may look weird, but I have found that it's not unusual for the different brands of monitors to vary up to 10 bpm.

Related Consumer Products

Accessories to heart rate monitors are proliferating as enhancements to the hardware are developed. Computer programs, books, newsletters, pamphlets, harnesses for swimmers, mounting brackets, extra-long chest straps (endurance horse people are using the hardware to train their animals), extra small chest straps for children and other small animals are just some of them. Several manufacturers have developed interface systems that allow you to download the data into a computer for analysis either immediately or later. One manufacturer using infrared telemetry gives you a continuous color readout with calories burned and heart rate displayed. It's all a question of needs and wants and where these intersect with what's practical for you.

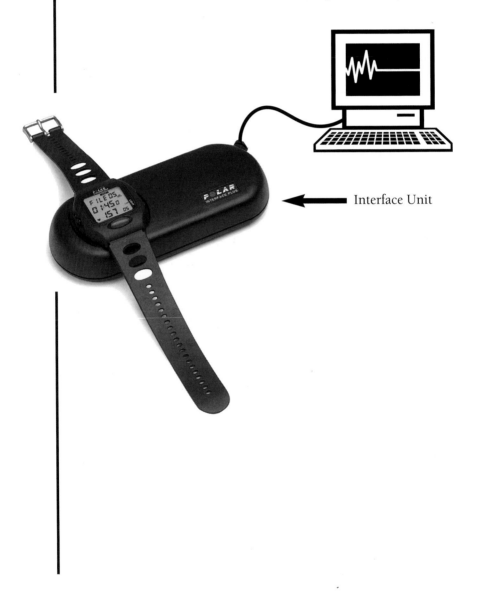

Interface Unit

Glossary
of Terms

Adaptation: the process of physiological change which occurs when the body responds to the stresses of training loads.

Aerobic: with or in the presence of oxygen; an exercise program at a low enough intensity to keep you and your muscles from running out of oxygen.

Aerobic capacity: the ability of the body to remove oxygen from the air and transfer it through the lungs and blood to the working muscles.

Anaerobic: without oxygen; exercise characterised by short-spurt, high-intensity activities where the muscles briefly operate at an oxygen deficit.

Anaerobic threshold: the point at which your body is producing more lactic acid than can be metabolised; also known as the "lactate threshold."

Base: a training term for the fitness level required to exercise for a relatively extended duration without tiring.

Calorie: the amount of heat necessary to raise the temperature of 1 gram of water one degree centigrade.

Carbohydrates: organic compounds which, when broken down, become a main energy source for muscular work and one of the basic food stuffs.

Cardiac: pertaining to the heart.

Cardiac cycle: one heart beat which includes the contraction and rest phase of the "Q-R-S-T" wave.

Cardiac deceleration: the slowing of your heart rate; cardiac acceleration is the increase in heart rate.

Catabolism: the breaking down of body tissue known as the destructive phase of metabolism; breakdown of chemical compounds.

Cross-over points: those heart rates where your metabolism shifts fuels, i.e., from burning fats to carbohydrates.

Electrocardiogram (EKG or ECG): a graphic record of electrical activity and heart beat pattern.

Fatigue: a diminished capacity for work as a result of long, hard exertion.

Fats: concentrated sources of energy for muscular work. They are compounds containing glycerol and fatty acids and may be saturated or unsaturated.

Heart rate: the number of beats or contraction cycles your heart makes per minute, measured by the electrical impulses emitted by the heart during this process.

HDL: high-density lipoproteins that return unused fat to the liver for disposal; cardiovascular type exercise raises HDL levels, which is beneficial to health because of the "removal" effect on harmful lipoproteins.

Ideal State of Excitability: that level of excitability when the individual is emotionally charged to perform to their best.

Intensity: degree of energy, difficulty, or strength, as relates to a workout.

Intervals: alternating periods of higher intensity with periods of lower intensity or recovery time workouts.

Lactic acid: this product of the body's metabolic processes is created during all of the heart rate zones, and is shuttled away from the skeletal muscles to different parts of the body where it is oxidised.

Microcycle: a training period of 7 to usually about 21 days in which a certain training regimen is followed.

Maximum Heart Rate: the greatest number of beats per minute possible for your heart; this number is highly individualised and varies with fitness, age, gender, and other factors. It is also sports specific.

Metabolism: the chemical changes in the body's cells by which energy is provided for vital processes.

Mitochondria: strings of carrier molecules within the cell; they act like tiny energy factories, taking fuel and uniting it with oxygen for combustion in the muscles.

Overuse: training too hard, to the point of stress or injury.

Polyunsaturated fat: a triglyceride in which the fatty acids have two or more points of unsaturation. Contains linoleic acid, an essential nutrient found in vegetable fats.

Pulse: the regular throbbing felt in the arteries which is caused by the contractions of the heart. This is not the same as electrically measured heart rate.

Resting heart rate: the number of heartbeats per minute when the body is at complete rest, usually determined upon awakening, but before arising.

Strength: maximum force or tension that a muscle can produce against resistance.

Training: any sustained cardiovascular exercise at a heart rate or intensity level sufficient to result in metabolic adaptation in the muscles involved. The commonly accepted lower threshold or floor for training is considered to be 50% of maximum heart rate.

Volume: the amount of training load as measured by time and distance per time, such as running 25 miles a week, but not using intensity as a factor.

VO$_2$ Max: the maximum volume of oxygen that the body can utilise, regardless of intensity increases; it is synonymous with "maximum oxygen consumption" and "maximum oxygen uptake."

Workload: the total training volume as measured by training frequency, intensity and duration as in the F.I.T. formula.

GLOSSARY OF HEART RATE TERMS

Ambient Heart Rate: the number of beats per minute your heart contracts when you are awake but in a sedentary and stationary position.

Anticipatory Heart Rate: a state of excitability in anticipation of an event in which heart rate normally increases.

Anaerobic Threshold Heart Rate: that heart rate at the moment when there is balance between anaerobic and aerobic metabolism.

Cross Over Point Heart Rate: that heart rate number when half of the fuels used for metabolism are from fat sources and half of the fuels used are from carbohydrates. This number shifts with fitness such that a higher percentage of fat is burned at lower heart rate values.

Delta Heart Rate: a test which measures the heart rate difference between lying prone and standing. The lower the difference the fitter and less stressed is the individual

Heart Rate Functions: the different features that the heart rate watch provides, such as the ability to display current heart rate.

Heart Rate Monitor: an electronic device which measures the electrical activity of the heart and displays it.

Heart Rate Watch: an electronic device which combines a time of day watch with the features of a heart rate monitor in one unit.

Heart Zones: different heart rate ranges which represent specific benefits that occur by exercising or training within their numeric limits.

Lactate Threshold Heart Rate: same as anaerobic threshold heart rate.

Limits: the dividing lines of a heart zone - the top of a limit is the ceiling and the lowest point of a limit is its floor.

 Maximum Heart Rate: the highest number of contractions of the heart muscle in one minute.

Maximum Sustainable Heart Rate: the highest steady state heart rate that can be sustained over an extended period of time.

Midpoint Heart Rate: that heart rate number which is in the middle of a heart zone.

Peak Heart Rate: highest heart rate during any one workout period.

Recovery Heart Rate: the number of beats per minute your heart drops after exercise, usually measured after two minutes of rest. See also p.13.

Resting Heart Rate: the number of beats your heart contracts in sixty seconds when you first wake up, before you get out of bed.

Steady State Heart Rate: that heart rate which is held at the same number throughout the exercise period.

Threshold Heart Rate: same as anaerobic threshold heart rate.

VO_2 Max HR: the heart rate number at the time that VO2 maximum is reached.

Zone Floor Heart Rate: the heart rate number which is the lowest number in any of the five different zones.

Zone Ceiling Heart Rate: the heart rate number which is the highest number in any one of the five different zones.

RECOMMENDED READING

Technical Information:

Training Lactate Pulse Rate. Janssen, Peter. Polar Electro Oy, 1987.

Medicine in Sports Training and Coaching. Karger. Medicine and Sport Science vol. 35. International Council of Sport Science and Physical Education. 1992.

Guidelines for Exercise Testing and Prescription. Fifth Edition. Lea & Febiger. American College of Sports Medicine. 1995.

Physiological Assessment of Human Fitness, Foster, Karl and Maud, Peter J. Human Kinetics, 1995.

Heart Rate Training Books:

The Heart Rate Monitor Book. Sally Edwards, Polar Electro Oy, 1992.

Heart Zone Training. Sally Edwards, Adams Media, 1996.

Heart Monitor Training For the Complete Idiot. John L. Parker, Jr. Cedar Winds Publishing Company, 1993.

Scientific Heart Rate Training. Neil Craig & Michael Nunan, 1996.

Heart Rate Fitness Program for Australian Schools. Jenny Williams & Rae Nunan, 1997.

Heart Rate Training for Horses. Neil Craig & Michael Nunan, 1998.

Precision Training. Jon Ackland, Reid Books, New Zealand, 1998.

Precision Heart Rate Training. Edmund Burke, Human Kinetics, 1998.

Heart Zone Training for Health and Physical Education. Deve Swainn with Sally Edwards, Heart Zones, 1999.

Lessons from the Heart. Beth Kirkpatrick & Burton Birnbaum, Human Kinetics, 1997.

 Happy Reading!

NOTES